The Shocking
Book
of Records

GW00634455

Did you know that:

A mosquito has forty-seven teeth?

All polar bears are left-handed?

When the first escalator was installed at Harrods at the turn of the century, brandy was served to travellers when they reached the top in case they felt faint?

The only person known to have physically exploded to death was a twenty-six-year-old Dane, whose stomach burst open during an operation when a doctor's surgically-heated knife caused gases inside the body to ignite?

Early in 1958 *Life* magazine printed a nine-page interview with the Devil?

On 14 May 1936 Lina Medina gave birth to a healthy, bouncing baby in Lima, Peru. The mother was aged five years and eight months at the time?

Martin Guinness

The Shocking
Book
of Records

Cartoons by Harry North

SPHERE BOOKS LIMITED
30-32 Gray's Inn Road, London WC1X 8JL

Contents

Anything You Can Do

'Most people have seen worse things in private than they pretend to be shocked at in public.'

Edgar Watson Howe

How long was Napoleon's penis? How many lovers did Catherine the Great have? What is the greatest recorded number of ejaculations enjoyed by any one person in a single night? Who was the world's most unsuccessful gambler? Which Pope took a sixteen-year-old mistress when he was pushing sixty-three? Who is the man that spent eighty-one whole years in prison and why? Which French prince was brought up as a girl and led his troops into battle wearing high heels? Who was history's highest paid hit-man? Is it true that Marie Antoinette and Jayne Mansfield shared identical bust measurements? Who is the world's most extravagant lover?

These and hundreds of similar questions have puzzled me for a long time, and yet amazingly enough the alluring and arresting answers are not readily available in any standard reference book. Visit your local library and ask the assistant if it is true that Rasputin's erect penis measured thirteen inches, and not only will you need to go armed with a large dose of smelling salts, but you will have to prepare yourself for being arrested for insulting behaviour, or at the very least a bucketful of cold water.

If you are interested in the more intimate details of the famous, the infamous and the totally unknown, then at long last here is the book you have been waiting for. *The Shocking Book of Records* will do for the reference book what *The Tropic of Cancer* did for marine navigation. From the intimate private lives of figures as diverse as St Augustine and Roman Polanski to the scarcely credible debauchery of Augustan Rome and Hogarthian London, from the private indulgences of Samuel Pepys and Adolf Hitler to the wildest profligacies of the Marquis de Sade and Gabriele D'Annunzio, ALL has been revealed.

Leaving behind me a trail of blushing librarians, embarrassed historians, red-faced scientists, and a vast number of totally bewildered members of the medical profession, I have collected together a unique collection of fantastic and fascinating facts of life, so shamefully ignored by other compilers of reference books. You won't find facts and figures about South American root crops, North American energy consumption, West Indian batting averages or Europe's tallest triplets – but you will discover some of the most interesting information ever recorded, the most hair-raising, sado-masochistic, intimate, scandalous and criminal records that have to be seen to be believed.

If you happen to be of a nervous disposition, have the constitution of a maiden aunt, and find it impossible to undress with the light on, then you have most certainly picked up the wrong book. But if you've always wanted to know that, after measles, VD is the second greatest health hazard in Barnet, or that one of the most exclusive clubs is the 20,000 club, members all being able to boast that they have had sex in an airplane at 20,000 feet, or that Jack the Ripper was left-handed, then prepare yourself for a shock . . .

Beginning at the Beginning

'Every public action which is not customary, either is wrong or, if it is right, is a dangerous precedent. It follows that nothing should be done for the first time.'

F. M. Cornford

The first experiments with artificial insemination were carried out in 1885 by a priest called Lazzaro Spallanzi when he successfully fertilised a dog. He was the first person to investigate sperm and the first to claim that semen was necessary for fertilisation.

*

The first blood transfusions used animals' blood, and during the Second World War when there was a shortage of blood it was found that milk from young coconuts is a good substitute for blood plasma.

*

Before the introduction of anaesthetics, any kind of operation was like deliberate and unendurable torture. At the beginning of the nineteenth century nitrous oxide, laughing gas, was found to have anaesthetic properties and was first used in 1844 for dental operations.

*

Local anaesthetics to numb pain during operations were used as early as 140 AD in China, and physician Hua T'o used to render his patients totally unconscious with alcohol.

*

Although reminiscent of a Science Fiction film, the first *head* transplants have already been performed in Cleveland, Ohio. Such experiments have so far proved to be successful, but fortunately have only been attempted on monkeys.

*

The first antibiotic, Penicillin, was actually discovered by accident in 1928 when mould landed in an experimental dish of culture and was found to have killed the bacteria present. Early antibiotics, however, were used in ancient Egypt, for sick people were given mouldy bread to cure them. It took 2000 more years for doctors to realise the significance of this cure.

When André-Jacques Garnerin landed after making the first parachute descent in 1797 the first thing he did was to vomit violently.

*

The first flush toilet on record is one discovered during excavations in Crete at the end of the last century. This highly advanced piece of plumbing in the palace of Knossos is over 4000 years old.

*

The first artificial hand was developed by a Frenchman in 1551. Ambroise Paré produced a hand made of cogs and levers that allowed a handless person to ride a horse by clasping the reins.

Doorkeeper, Antonie van Leeuwenhoek, in the seventeenth century at the Delft City Hall, spent his spare time experimenting with tiny lenses and built his own microscope. He became the first person to study human spermatozoa and was able to describe it in great detail.

*

Paper was first invented in China in 105 AD by Ts'ai Lun, a eunuch – the only eunuch to go down in the history of technology.

*

The first contraceptive diaphragms were made from orange peel. Half an orange was sufficient.

*

Dr Rene Läennec (1781-1826) unwittingly produced the first stethoscope. When confronted with a very plump patient he found that he could not hear her heartbeat, so he rolled up a tube of paper and placed one end between her breasts and the other end to his ear. It worked!

*

When the first escalator was installed at Harrods department store at the turn of the century, brandy was served to travellers when they reached the top in case they felt faint!

*

Jimmy Carter was the first and only President of the United States to have been born in a hospital. All other Presidents have been born 'at home'.

*

A man named Palmer constructed the first stocks in Boston in 1634, and then became the first person to occupy them for charging too high a price for making them. He was charged with profiteering.

The first contraceptive sheaths were used by the Romans, and were usually made of sheep's intestines.

*

The first snow in the Sahara desert fell in living memory when a half-hour snowstorm occurred on February 18, 1978. But within a short time the snow had completely disappeared.

*

Minnie Dean became the first woman to be hanged in New Zealand when she was executed on 12 August, 1895. For six years she had adopted unwanted babies for a fee and then killed them. She buried their bodies in her flower garden.

*

The first birth recorded in Antarctica took place on 7 January, 1978, at an army base.

*

The first fish in space was a South American guppie. It spent forty-eight days in orbit in 1976 on a Russian Salyut 5 spaceship.

*

One of the first charges at the first hearing of the first juvenile court was 'shouting celery in the street'.

*

The first record of a murder trial is of one held at Sumer in 1700 BC.

*

The first conviction made in Britain on fingerprint evidence was against Harry Jackson, accused of stealing billiard balls in June 1902.

The first female students were adopted by the great Philosopher, Epicurus, in around 300 BC. Sex equality is not a modern innovation!

*

The first capital punishment in the British Isles took place in 450 AD. By the reign of Edward VI an average of 560 executions took place at Tyburn alone every year.

*

The first hydrogen bomb, tested in 1952, was said to be more powerful than the total of all the bombs dropped on Japan and Germany during the Second World War, which includes the atomic bombs dropped on Nagasaki and Hiroshima.

*

The first sex-change operation was performed on 1 December, 1952, when George Jorgenson, ex-armed forces, was surgically transformed into a woman.

*

The world's first testicle transplant was performed in St Louis, when Timothy Twomey who had no testicles received a testicle from his identical twin, Terry. Both were fertile and able to produce sperm normally. Such an operation is rarely performed because it is only feasible for identical twins to have testicle transplants. Men with one testicle can, however, have a non-functioning artificial testicle inserted into the scrotal sack, but this is purely for cosmetic reasons. The normal healthy male can have a perfectly normal sex life with only one testicle.

*

The first glue was made by the Romans, who boiled together such substances as blood, milk, bones, and even mistletoe juice. Their aim? To catch birds by spreading branches of trees with glue, so that when the bird sat on the branch it remained stuck. This was their theory anyway . . . .

A woman called Zazel became the first human cannonball on 2 April, 1877, when she was shot a distance of sixty feet at London's Westminster Aquarium. For this act of daring she earnt £120 a week.

*

Numerous hairstyles have been created this century alone, but Scottish hairdresser, Melvin Wood, created the very first tartan hairstyle. It cost £110 and took almost twenty hours to perform, with over twenty different dyes being used. One person to have a less elaborate version of this style was personality Jimmy Savile.

Mary Phelps Jacob, pained by her whalebone corsets, invented the first brassière in 1914.

*

The first advertisement on commercial radio was for a laxative.

Crime, Cruelty and Corruption

'A good man can be stupid and still be good.
But a bad man must have brains – absolutely.'

Maxim Gorky

A statistical study by the British Fire Research Station showed that the average arsonist was a male teenager, and most likely to strike seven days after the new moon.

*

In 1831 a boy of nine was hanged for arson.

*

There have only been thirteen convictions made from over 1000 Chicago murders committed in the last sixty years.

*

In the last fifty years in our 'civilised' society, a human being has been killed every twenty seconds.

*

Every year in the USA some 40,000,000 people are murdered, raped, or mugged.

In 1348 eighty-eight cases of murder were recorded in Yorkshire. A modern equivalent in England and Wales would not be less than 10,000 a year. Even today more murders appear to take place in Yorkshire than in any other county – in recent years the 'Yorkshire Ripper' being the most notorious.

Imprisoning criminals is a fairly recent innovation. In years gone by a hand or foot was chopped off as punishment for the crime, or at worst the head, and such barbaric forms of punishment still exist in countries like Saudi Arabia.

*

In ancient India a punishment for adultery was to cut off the person's nose. Early forms of plastic surgery were later performed on the unfortunate victims when pieces of skin were taken from the middle of their forehead and sewn where their nose once was. Possibly the earliest skin grafts.

*

Notorious Chicago gangster, O'Banion, was wiped out of existence by Al Capone. O'Banion was then given the largest funeral ever known for a gangster, and the most expensive wreath which cost over 1000 dollars. It was from Al Capone.

*

Only a mother can be charged with infanticide. Any other parties are charged with murder.

*

The strangest crime for which anyone has ever been fined must be that of kissing a traffic warden's elbow whilst she is giving you a parking ticket. In 1976 a twenty-four-year-old man in Oklahoma, USA, was charged, convicted of assault and fined 200 dollars for this very offence.

*

Colombia has the highest recorded murder rate with over 300,000 murders in one seventeen-year period (1945-62), which works out at approximately forty-eight murders a day.

*

The Argentinian police were the first to adopt the use of fingerprints to investigate crimes.

The luckiest criminal must be John Smith, a condemned robber who in 1705 was hanged and dangled on the end of the rope for fifteen minutes. He was cut down and found to still be alive. He was reprieved.

*

Buhram, a member of the violent Indian thuggee sect, strangled over 900 people in fifty years.

*

The most prolific 'one-at-a-time' murderer in the twentieth century was the German Bruno Lüdke, who between 1928 and 1943 killed eighty-five women. He confessed to this crime, and was put to death himself without trial in April 1944.

*

Bodies of victims murdered by arsenic turn a characteristic mahogany colour.

*

The youngest person to have been kidnapped was Carolyn Wharton. Born at 12.46 pm on 19 March, 1955 in Texas, USA, she was kidnapped twenty-nine minutes later by a woman disguised as a nurse.

*

The greatest computer fraud occurred on the computer of the Equity Funding Corporation when, between 1964 and 1973, nearly 65,000 fake insurance policies were put on the computer and swindled the company out of 2,000,000,000 dollars.

*

The last prisoner to be held in the Tower of London was the Nazi leader Rudolph Hess who was imprisoned there during the Second World War.

Jean de Sperati was the most famous philatelic forger of all time. By 1953 he had produced between fifty and seventy thousand forged stamps with his unique knowledge of photography and printing.

*

Arthur Ferguson, in 1924, conned American tourists into buying Big Ben for £1000 and Nelson's Column for £6000, and even managed to get one man to put a down payment on Buckingham Palace.

*

Twenty-six Popes have been assassinated.

*

Over 30,000 serious sexual offences take place in England and Wales annually.

*

Theft is the biggest crime in Great Britain with more than one-and-a-half million individual cases every year.

*

The greatest robbery ever known was in May 1945 when 400,000,000 dollars was taken from a German bank.

*

The oldest person to be hanged for murder in the United Kingdom was Charles Frembd aged seventy-one, who was hanged at Chelmsford gaol in 1914 for the murder of his wife.

*

Fortune tellers are still liable to punishment under section four of the 1824 Vagrancy Act.

According to a professional hangman a person weighing 50.8 kg (8 st) requires a drop of 3.04 m (10 ft), 0.6 m (2 ft) longer than that required for someone weighing 88.9 kg (14 st).

*

Homosexual John Wayne Gacy, aged thirty-seven, was sentenced to death by the electric chair on 13 March, 1980 for the murder of thirty-three men, making America's greatest mass murderer of men. The thirty-three corpses were found under the floorboards of his home.

*

The cleverest and most ingenious prison escape on record is that of a one-legged thief in Lescar, France, who managed to break out of his cell using his steel false leg to undo the door bolts.

The macabre record of Britain's greatest female mass killer still belongs to Mary Ann Cotton (b.1832) who killed twenty-one people, many of them children, with arsenic before she was brought to the notice of the police and the so-called 'natural' deaths were investigated. She was sentenced to death and hanged in March 1873, maintaining her innocence to the end – despite the fact that traces of arsenic were found to be in the stomachs of all her victims.

*

The most notorious unknown murderer in history must undoubtedly be the nineteenth century killer known as Jack the Ripper. In 1888 five prostitutes in Whitechapel in the East End of London were slashed, mutilated and dissected, in some of the most horrific murders recorded. The contents of their bodies and internal organs were literally splattered around the room, and on one occasion 'the Ripper' taunted the police by sending them the half-eaten kidney of Catherine Eddowes, one of his victims. Despite numerous theories and suspects, the killer was never caught. One theory was that Queen Victoria's grandson, the Duke of Clarence, was the murderer, whilst a more recent revelation is that Jack the Ripper was not one person but a gang of three men, which is why such bloodthirsty slaughters took place in so short a time and remained undetected. Probably we shall never know.

*

The most unusual thief was a Turk who managed to rob an electrical shop in Ilford, Essex. He gave the proprietor of the shop a £20 note that had chloroform on it. By the time he had regained consciousness, the thief had made off with nearly £2000 from the till.

The most ambitious crime recorded is that of the theft of a house. In 1971 number 10, Jardin Street, London, was removed brick by brick over a period of time, and was presumably built somewhere else. The entire house totally disappeared.

*

Jean-Charles Willoquet was arrested by members of the French Anti-Gang squad. Willoquet was at home at the time of his arrest, seated in front of his TV set – watching a documentary about . . . the French Anti-Gang squad.

Death, Doom and Disaster

'There's nothing certain in a man's
life but this:
That he must lose it.'

Earl of Lytton

According to official figures there is one suicide every twenty minutes in the USA.

*

The most intense earthquake happened in the United States in 1811 when more than one million square miles suffered under the tremor. The course of the Mississippi was changed as a result and shocks were felt more than 1000 miles away.

*

The last public execution by the guillotine occurred as late as June 1939 when murderer Eugen Weidmann lost his head in Paris at 4.50 am on the seventeenth of that month.

*

A survey shows that more than fifty per cent of the population die within three months of their birth date.

*

One of the worst coalmining disasters happened in 1906 at the Courrières coal mine in France, when more than 1000 miners were killed.

*

In the middle of the fourteenth century seventy-five million people died as a result of the Black Death, which is one in four of the population in Europe.

*

The greatest natural disaster happened in 1970 when a tropical cyclone hit East Pakistan in November of that year, causing the deaths of more than one million people.

*

The polygamous Thracian people of 1300-500 BC went through a great ritual when a warrior died. His many wives argued as to who had been his special favourite so that she could be killed and buried with him. The wives fought tooth and nail to achieve this high honour.

*

The worst steamship accident took place in April 1865, when soldiers from the Civil War, anxious to get home, crowded onto the steamboat *Sultana*. The boilers exploded, killing 1700 men.

*

Deer hunter, Endre Bascany, did the best impression of a stag's mating call. He was shot dead by another deer hunter.

*

The greatest sea disaster of all time was not the sinking of the *Titanic*, in which 1513 lives were lost, but the sinking of the German ship *Wilhelm Gustloff* in 1945. Almost 8000 people drowned.

*

More than 400 people are killed by lightning every year in America, more than any other natural disaster. It is also a fallacy that lightning doesn't strike twice, because it always follows the path of least resistance – which is likely to be a path it has taken before!

*

Fifty per cent of the people who die in Britain are now cremated.

*

Welshman, Griffith Morgan, was one of the fastest runners of his time (born 1696). In 1732 he ran twelve miles in fifty-three minutes, and received one hundred gold sovereigns as a prize. Anxious to congratulate Morgan, someone slapped him on the back in a friendly gesture. He fell down dead. Nothing like quitting while you're on top!

Pope Leo VIII died of a heart attack whilst committing adultery.

*

The first recorded case of death by yoga is that of twenty-nine-year-old American, Robert Antosczyck, who went into a deep trance, slowing his heart down so much that it stopped. He died in the lotus position.

*

The most disastrous plane crash in the history of aviation was the collision of two jumbo jets in Tenerife on 27 March, 1977. Unbelievably the accident happened *on the ground* when the two taxiing planes collided killing 580 people.

*

Thirty thousand people died in the earthquake which hit the city of St Pierre on the Caribbean island of Martinique in 1908. The only survivor was a short-term prisoner in the city's gaol.

Frau Irmgard Brens, a nineteenth century citizen of Berlin, was widowed six times – all her husbands committed suicide.

*

The busiest morgue is in the Bronx, New York. On occasions next of kin have had to wait in queues and are given numbers so that they can await their body-identification call.

*

Until 1823 the bodies of suicides were always buried in unconsecrated ground, and to prevent the bodies from rising and haunting the neighbourhood, a wooden stake was driven through the heart, pinning the corpse to the ground in an effort to stop it moving. A murderer in St John's Wood became the last corpse to be staked in this manner.

*

The sixth most common form of accidental death in America is that of choking. More than 2500 people die each year by getting food caught in their throats, and the foods that the majority choke on are surprisingly bread and hard boiled eggs.

*

The greatest mass suicide took place in Guyana on 18 November, 1978, when 910 people poisoned themselves with cyanide.

*

The greatest disaster in the history of the circus was on 6 July, 1944 when a circus tent in Hartford, Connecticut, caught fire and 168 people were burnt to death in the resulting inferno. A further 600 people sustained injuries.

*

The only person known to have physically exploded to death was a twenty-six-year-old Dane, whose stomach burst open during an operation when a doctor's surgically-heated knife caused gases inside the body to ignite.

*

On 2 February, 1556 the worst earthquake *ever* occurred in China, killing 830,000 people.

*

Drinking yourself to death seems quite a common suicide when you think of the destructive effects of alcohol, but a Miami woman managed to drink herself to death with water. She drank so much water that she virtually drowned on dry land and her lungs filled with water.

*

Around 1820, 176 blacks were taken prisoner during a revolt on San Domingo and were locked up for the night. The following morning, 173 of them were found to have committed suicide by throttling themselves to death.

*

In 1976 one in ten men who died in Britain died of cancer. In the United States one person dies of cancer every ninety seconds.

*

Every year in the United States more than 50,000 deaths are caused by car accidents. One single airplane crash makes headline news all round the world, and yet the millions of people killed by cars around the world every year seem to be forgotten.

*

In the nineteenth century poor families gave their children a mixture known as 'Godfrey's Cordial'. It was made from treacle, sassafras and opium and caused a quick, painless death when the children became too expensive to feed.

Radical feminist, Victoria Woodhull, felt that being old she would die if she laid down in a bed. She spent the last four years of her life sitting in her chair, dying just before her ninetieth birthday.

*

In Japan it is impossible legally to buy a gun. The murder rate in Japan is 200 times less than that of America where a gun is bought every thirteen seconds.

*

Doctors kill themselves at twice the rate of average men. This is thought to be because of the great stress and responsibility that the job entails. The percentage of female doctors who commit suicide is said to be sixty per cent higher than that of women in other professions.

*

Suicides are most likely to occur in spring or summer, in the afternoon rather than the evening or morning, during peacetime and when there is high unemployment.

Eccentrics, Evils and Ecclesiastics

'It is no accident that the symbol
of a Bishop is a crook, and the sign of
an Archbishop is a double cross.'

Dom Gregory Dix

Eccentric artist, Dennis Oppenheimer, took one of the most unusual photographs in 1970. It was entitled *Reading Position for a Second Degree Burn*, and the artist posed for it himself. He lay naked in the sun with an open book spread across his chest for many hours until his skin began to burn. A photograph was then taken of his badly burned body with a white rectangle of unexposed flesh on his chest.

*

As late as 1942 Wilbur Glenn Volvia was asserting that the 'earth is as flat as a pancake'.

*

The Potsdam Grenadiers were the unique army of Frederick the Great, made up of above average height men. He collected together as many 'giant' men and women as he could, hoping to breed a nation of giants. It didn't work.

*

St Catherine's monastery near Mount Sinai is stacked with the skulls of Greek Orthodox monks, the earliest dating from the second century AD. This is because St Catherine's is a holy place, reputed to be built on the spot where God spoke to Moses from the burning bush, and even today the local monks request that their heads be added to the pile when they die.

*

Victorian advocate of cremation, Dr William Price, stated in his will that he wanted to be cremated in public. His body was burned on a hill top and over 20,000 people turned up to watch.

*

Showman P. T. Barnum included in his entourage some Red Indians, who performed an authentic wedding ceremony twice daily in his show. Part of the ceremony involves the giving of a red blanket to the bride's father, and the Indians demanded a brand new blanket for each 'wedding' and would never use the same one twice. The blankets cost ten dollars each, which meant Barnum had to fork out an extra twenty dollars a day. The Indians did not remain in the show for long!

*

Religious 'perfectionists' called the Oneida, a sect in New York, claimed that sexual pleasure and actual copulation should be separated. The women of the sect taught the young boys how to withhold orgasm. The men taught the young girls.

*

When having his hair cut Howard Hughes insisted that the barber use three dozen combs and specified that he should use new scissors made of German soligen steel.

*

In 1909 Robert Hardie, a London barber, shaved six men in one minute and then blindfolded he shaved another man in twenty-seven seconds. It is not recorded whether or not his 'victims' were cut up about it!

In 1765, a brewer's assistant, Walter Willey, devoured in a public house in Aldersgate Street, London, a roast goose weighing six pounds, a loaf of bread, and three quarts of port for a wager with no ill effect. His meal took one hour eight minutes.

*

Zoroaster, the famous Persian lawgiver and founder of the Parsee religion, lived on nothing but cheese for fifty years.

*

An Austrian named Johann Hurlinger walked from Vienna to Paris on his hands in fifty-five days. His average speed over the 1400 km (871 miles) journey was slightly over 2.5 km/h (1½ mph).

*

In 1565, at the age of nineteen, astronomer Tycho Brahe took part in a duel over a mathematical argument. The result was that Tycho lost his nose. For the remainder of his life he wore a false nose made of metal.

Angelique Cottin was an extraordinary fourteen-year-old French girl with record breaking powers. She could knock over heavy pieces of furniture just by touching them gently, and anyone shaking hands with her received an electric shock.

*

Blackbird, Chief of the Ohama Indian tribe, requested that when he died he was buried astride his favourite horse. His wish was carried out.

*

A seventeenth century chancellor of Cambridge University, Dr Lightfoot, claimed that God completed the act of creation at 9.00 am on 23 October, 4004 BC.

*

The most extreme measure taken to get a child to speak occurred when five-year-old Arshile Gorky refused to talk after the break-up of his parents' marriage. He remained completely mute until one day he saw his teacher leap over a cliff. The child cried out in horror. It was only a stunt on the part of the teacher, but it cured the child.

*

Eccentric actress, Sarah Bernhardt, had an obsession about death and liked nothing better in her leisure time than to spend a few hours in the Paris morgue studying the corpses. Towards the end of her life she frequently slept in a rosewood coffin, and always kept it at the foot of her bed. When she eventually died she was buried in it, so it came in useful after all!

*

A twenty-one-year-old woman took the Bible literally, and chopped off her own hand when she felt that she had sinned. She arrived at the hospital carrying the hand in a polythene bag quoting the passage: 'Wherefore if thy hand or thy foot

offend thee, cut them off and cast them from thee.'
Fortunately doctors were able to sew the hand back on again.

*

A twenty-four-year-old man made an attempt at jumping
Minnesota's forty-foot wide Lacque Park river on a
motorised lawn mower. He missed . . . by thirty-five feet.

*

The Parsee religious community of India believe that the
souls of their dead will reach heaven quicker if their bodies are
picked clean of flesh. The bodies of the deceased are,
therefore, placed high up on a long pole or tower, and the
Parsees pray whilst vultures make a meal of their departed
relative. Not a pretty sight!

*

The artist Pablo Picasso had a unique way of keeping warm.
He set fire to his early paintings.

*

Early in 1958 *Life* magazine printed a nine-page interview
with the Devil.

*

The richest American ever known, Andrew Carnegie,
became allergic to money in his old age. He never carried any
with him and claimed that he couldn't bear the sight of it. He
was frequently thrown out of restaurants and taxis because he
was unable to pay the bill, and yet he was a multi-millionaire!

*

In 1783, eighteen-year-old Charles Byrne died having
attained a height of seven feet. John Hunter had a desire to
own Byrne's body and illegally paid the undertakers £500 for
it – the highest price ever paid for a human body.

Having won the Los Angeles *Housewife of the Year* competition, one Mrs Cros was given the choice of any prize she wanted. She asked to blow something up with dynamite!

*

The strangest fashion is that of the Indian Chinook tribe. They feel that it is beautiful to have a flat skull, and so strap their babies' heads to a piece of board for the first twelve months of their life to give them the desired look.

*

The Roman Emperor Caligula was the first, and only, person to make his horse a consul.

*

Nathan Coker was a blacksmith in the State of Maryland well suited to his trade. He could hold a white-hot shovel against his bare foot until it cooled; he used to swill molten lead around his mouth until that solidified and he could lift red-hot iron from the furnace with his bare hands.

*

'Liver-eating' Johnston attained infamy by eating the livers of Crow Indians that he killed. The Indians murdered Johnston's wife and this was his way of getting revenge. The fact that livers are rich in iron probably accounts for the fact that he lived to be nearly eighty.

*

Filled with a morbid curiosity thousands of people had a day excursion to Palmetto, Georgia, in 1899 to witness a lynching. Many people bought home slices of the victim's body as a permanent souvenir of the day out.

In 1883 a Chinese priest in Shanghai decided to grow his finger nails; twenty-seven years later they were 58 cm (22.8 in) long.

*

The Roman poet Virgil once spent over £50,000 on the funeral of a pet fly, the highest recorded amount paid out for the funeral of a pet.

ood Glorious Food

'The French are fond of slugs and frogs
The Siamese eat puppy dogs
And all the world is torn and rent
By varying views on nutriment.'

Hilaire Belloc

'Jack Sprat could eat no fat
His wife could eat no lean –
A real sweet pair of neurotics.'

Jack Sharkey

The average person consumes 23.6 pounds of breakfast cereal every year. The greatest producer of breakfast cereals is, of course, Kellogg's – a name synonymous with breakfast – who produce one-and-a-half million packets of cereal every day.

*

The Aztec's highest source of protein in their diet came from eating human corpses. More than a quarter of a million people, that's one per cent of the population, were sacrificed to the Gods annually. Obviously it seemed a pity to waste such good food, it would have been a sin . . .

*

A normal healthy adult could survive eight weeks without any food at all, providing water was drunk to prevent dehydration.

*

In Florida rattlesnake meat is served as an hors d'oeuvre.

*

The largest hen's egg was laid in Russia by a Soviet hen. It contained nine yolks, weighed fourteen ounces and was five and a half inches long.

*

The average adult consumes 2.4 kilowatts of energy from food every day. This is the equivalent of giving a car seven gallons of petrol.

*

In 1811 a blacksmith at Stroud, Gloucestershire, devoured for a small wager, one pint of periwinkles, complete with shells, in ten minutes. He then repeated the feat on request, and died.

One of the most popular delicacies in ancient Rome was roast dormouse.

*

The Roman upper classes used lead as a sweetener in food and as a cure for stomach upsets. They slowly poisoned themselves, women became infertile, and lead poisoning has been blamed as the major cause of the fall of the Roman Empire.

*

According to a recent survey there are nearly 30,000 different methods of losing weight. There is, however, only one really successful method of slimming – don't eat!

*

Within twenty years the amount of land used for the cultivation of spinach in the USA increased twenty-one times. This growth in the period between the wars also coincided with the advent of Popeye, the champion of spinach.

*

The first chewing gum was originally intended to be a rubber substitute – but it tasted nice.

*

The Spanish were the first to eat chocolate in Europe, the first being imported from Mexico in 1520. The first recorded chocolate factory to be opened in Britain was not until 1720.

*

The Chinese are the only race with a passion for eating dogs.

*

The greatest seller of hamburgers in the USA is McDonald's, who have sold on average twenty-five billion since the company began.

Chicken feathers are ninety-seven per cent protein and can be ground into a powder for cooking.

*

London's only horsemeat banquet took place at the Langham Hotel in 1868, when almost 300 people dined on 'Baron of horse'.

*

One of the most unusual gourmet events that takes place annually is the 'Live-minnow-eating contest' that takes place in Geraardsbergen, in Belgium. Although called 'minnow-eating', it is more accurate to call it 'drinking' because the live fish are placed in a large goblet of red wine, and then the wine is consumed.

*

In fifty years as a restaurant grader Fred Magel holds the record for having eaten in nearly 40,000 restaurants around the world.

*

A delicacy in Japan is the fu-gu fish. Tasty indeed, yet over 200 people die every year after eating fu-gu because the fish is poisonous. Unless prepared by highly skilled chefs who know exactly which parts of the fish to serve, the dish is fatal.

*

In Iraq you can eat snakes on any day of the week except Sunday.

*

One of the rarest delicacies in Britain are 'braised dormice'. Killed by electrocution (the least messy method of execution!) they are casseroled in red wine before being fried so that they are crispy and succulent.

It is often said that packaging is more expensive than the product and this is certainly the case with sardines. The oil in which the sardines are packed is far more costly than the sardines themselves, which is probably why they are always tightly packed . . . like sardines!

*

A delicacy in Africa is fried ants. These are fried without oil and served with rice.

*

'To dust thou art, and to dust thou shalt return' seems a good enough reason to eat it! The poorer people of the Southern United States do, it was revealed in *The Lancet* in 1978, actually eat earth and clay. It is said to be very good for the bowels and does contain some nutrients and minerals, although its taste is unlikely to be the most delicious on the menu.

*

Packaged frozen foods were the brainchild of Clarence Birdseye. He perfected his technique after studying fish which had been caught and frozen in $-50°F$ and left for several months before being thawed out and found to be still alive.

*

The greatest number of cooked worms ever eaten is twenty-eight, consumed by a Californian man, Rusty Rice, at a worm eating competition at Rialto College.

*

The winning recipe of the COOKING WITH WORMS competition, sponsored by the North American Bait Company was a dish called Earthworm Applesauce Surprise Cake. Sounds delicious!

The largest omelette from one single egg, sufficient to feed twelve men, would need an ostrich egg. An ostrich egg has the same volume as two dozen hen's eggs. To boil one would take approximately forty minutes, and around one and a half hours to hard boil one. A hard boiled ostrich egg could withstand the weight of a 127 kg (twenty stone) man standing on its shell without cracking.

*

The last words of eighteenth century politician, William Pitt, were: 'I think I could eat one of Bellamy's pork pies.' Then he died.

*

Americans eat 700,000,000 dollars worth of lettuce annually, the highest consumer of lettuce in the world.

*

Kangaroo meat is the only meat without cholesterol.

*

The most popular insects eaten by people are: grasshoppers, beetles, crickets, locusts, caterpillars, termites and ants.

*

In the Middle Ages eating potatoes was thought to give you syphillis.

*

After a skull injury in 1974, Fannie Meyer of Johannesburg daily drank 160 pints of water.

Studies in cannibalism reveal that a man weighing sixty-eight kilos has sufficient meat on his body to make a meal for seventy-five people. Who wants the parson's nose?

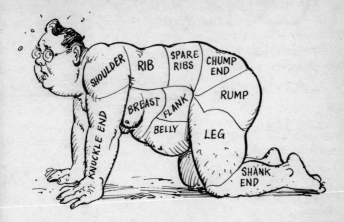

Marc Quinquadon in July 1979 obtained the world record for eating snails when he consumed 144 snails in eleven minutes thirty seconds, but on trying to beat the record four months later he collapsed and died after eating seventy-two snails in just three minutes (in itself a record, but not one that he can beat!).

*

In 1743 twelve-year-old Matthew Daking consumed 384 lb 2 oz (174,236 kg) of food in six days after contracting a rare disease known as *bulimia*, which causes the person to have a morbid desire to eat. The record has not been broken in almost 250 years.

Gay's the Word

'Their faces are so sad, but their bottoms are so gay.'

(Anon French Diplomat 1918)

Even if sperm banks had been around centuries ago, despite being geniuses the sperm of Michaelangelo and Leonardo da Vinci would have been rejected by Californian sperm banks because of their sexual preferences – the sperm bank consider homosexuality to be hereditary.

*

One man in twenty in Australia, Britain and the USA, and no doubt other Western countries, is exclusively homosexual; and one man in every ten has had a homosexual relationship of some duration.

*

In Britain today more than two million people are exclusively homosexual.

*

During the reign of Catherine I of Russia in the eighteenth century there was a law which stated that no woman must ever get drunk. To overcome this many thousands of young ladies revelled in transvestite balls and spent much of their time dressed as men.

*

Dr James Barry was a general in the army of Queen Victoria, and served as a surgeon for over forty years. It was not until his death in 1865 that his true sex was discovered. 'He' was a woman.

*

Rainer Maria Rilke, born 1875, one of Germany's greatest poets, spent the first six years of his life dressed as a girl because his mother wanted a daughter. He was known as 'Sophie'.

*

In 1962 one quarter of the States of America dropped their sodomy laws making it legal for the first time between consenting adults.

Otis Tabler, an American employee of the Department of Defence, became the first homosexual in 1975 to be entrusted with government secrets. This had previously been forbidden for fear of blackmail, but Tabler openly declared his homosexuality and so no longer became a security risk.

*

Contrary to popular belief only a very small percentage of lesbian woman use dildos or artificial penises during lovemaking.

*

In 1834 Sylvester Graham invented the 'Graham Cracker', a cereal food that was meant to curb sexual desire in gay men. Fifty years later John Harvey Kellogg began producing breakfast cereals in the same vein which were meant to curtail children's inclinations to masturbate.

*

Since World War II cases of venereal disease amongst gay men, (gonorrhea being the most common), have increased by 200 per cent.

*

In 1702 Lord Cornbury was appointed governor of New York and New Jersey in the American colonies. His lordship, a notorious transvestite, performed most of his official duties dressed as a woman and posed for his official portrait in a flattering evening gown.

*

In the Californian Gold Rush days, stagecoach driver Charlie Parkhurst drove shipments of gold down dangerous roads, smoked large cigars, shot highwaymen dead, and kept a cattle ranch. When he died in 1879 it was discovered for the first time that Charlie was a woman.

The only person ever to have served in the armed forces first as a man and later as a woman is Michael/Joanna Clark who served in the US navy as a man until 1969. After a sex-change in 1975 Joanna Clark rejoined the services, but this time went into the army.

*

Homosexual female rats have been seen to rub vaginas together, with one rat on top almost as if she had a penis, going through the same motions of heterosexual copulation.

*

A higher percentage of homosexuals become alcoholics than heterosexuals. This is in no way connected with any hang-ups or drinking to overcome problems, but because of the very nature of many gay lifestyles in which bars become the main meeting place for gay men.

*

A 1965 survey by the Institute for Sex Research at Indiana University revealed that only one in six gay men is easily recognisable as gay, the rest all act, dress, walk, look, and talk like straight men.

The Athenians considered male homosexuality to be the highest possible form of life because it was the only way a man could love an equal.

*

Fifty per cent of male homosexuals have had intercourse with women at some point in their lives, and seventy-five per cent of lesbians have had sex with a man.

*

A 1982 survey of homosexuality revealed that it has not increased in the last forty years, what *has* happened is that people now no longer feel that they need keep their sexuality secret.

*

In the USA the age of consent for homosexuals is sixteen in most states, but the lowest consenting age is twelve in Delaware, and fourteen in Hawaii.

*

One of the earliest countries to make homosexuality legal was France, where a law was passed in 1810.

*

In Spain imprisonment for up to eight years can be imposed on any suspected of having homosexual tendencies, so don't hold hands with your boyfriend next time you take a holiday in Barcelona!

*

A 150,000 franc prize was offered to anyone who could design a new uniform for the French army. Louis Feraud suggested embroidered uniforms with gold buttons, and real flowers on the helmet, along with bow ties, so that the soldiers would look 'much more gay' . . .

During the Second World War the Federal Bureau of Investigation (FBI) established a homosexual brothel of male prostitutes, which proved to be the most successful method of extracting information from foreign sailors.

History Repeats

'You don't have to be a Marxist to see
that history repeats itself,
first as a tragedy, then as a farce.'

Anon.

Many centuries ago the most used detergent was urine. It used throughout the world and it is known that the Romans had special 'public lavatories' for men in which all the urine was collected for washing togas and keeping them white. The major component of urine is ammonia, which is, of course, still used in many cleaning products today. Ninety-four per cent of urine is water anyway, so it was a very cheap form of washing detergent and readily available!

*

The bubonic plague or Black Death which killed some sixty million people in the fourteenth century is *still around*! In 1978 there were eleven cases in America, two of which were fatal.

*

In Biblical times and in ancient Rome it was the custom for a man when swearing the truth to place his right hand on his testicles. The word 'testimony' has entered our language as a result.

*

The Venerable Bede in AD 700 was the first person to start dating historical events from the birth of Christ.

*

The Cloaca Maxima, one of the great drains of Rome, was opened in 588 BC and is still in existence. In England the first public officials responsible for drains were not appointed until 1513, over 2000 years later.

*

To limit births, Elizabethan men did not marry until they were twenty-seven and the average bride was twenty-four. Presumably pre-marital sex and unmarried mothers were not considered a problem.

The largest hailstones ever known fell in Seringpatan, India, in 1870. They were said to be as large as elephants.

*

In the history of the world there have been ten years of war to every year of peace.

*

Demosthenes (380-322 BC) was said to be the greatest orator ever, yet as a child he had a speech impediment. He cured his own stammer by speaking with a mouthful of pebbles.

*

One of the most amazing remarks on record is credited to mathematician and philosopher, Blaise Pascal, who claimed that if Cleopatra's nose had been a different shape the history of the world would have been changed.

Spartans of Ancient Greece had to adhere to a law which said a man must marry by the age of thirty. If still bachelors they were not allowed to take part in nude orgies that were frequently held.

*

The pens with which the Treaty of American Independence was signed in 1782 realised £500 in an auction sale in London in 1891.

*

In the year 1800 a man could be sentenced to two hours in the stocks for kissing his wife in public on a Sunday. This was 'lewd and unseemly' behaviour and was a punishable offence.

*

In the 1980's a space rocket can now reach the moon in less time than it once took a stagecoach to travel the length of England.

*

When President John F. Kennedy was assassinated in 1963 it was not a federal felony to kill a president of the United States.

*

Kern, the architect who built the famous St Basil church in Moscow, had his eyes put out by Ivan the Terrible (1440-1505) in order to prevent him building a similar church elsewhere.

*

Passion for gin increased from two million to five million gallons a year between 1714-1733.

*

The winter of 1582 was the coldest on record in Vienna, and wolves were said to enter the city and attack humans and cattle.

Ingenious Inventions and Inventors

'Thus were they defiled with their own works and went a whoring with their own inventions.'

Psalm 106

Alfred Nobel, the Swedish donor of the Nobel Peace Prize, was the inventor of dynamite which has caused the death of more people than any other invention.

*

Alfred Nobel's father, Immanuel Nobel, was the inventor of plywood.

*

The first dentures were made by artist and innovator, Charles Wilson Peale, and were made out of elks teeth, set in lead. These false teeth were created for George Washington, who used to soak them in port to improve their flavour.

*

Chemist John Walker never patented his invention, which is now found in practically every household – matches.

*

The most ingenious invention for curing tension is Japanese. At the Matsushita Electric Company the workers are given dummies of their foreman and some bamboo sticks. At the end of a hard week they can take out all their aggression by physically beating these dummies. They then go home to the families for a relaxed weekend, having got rid of all their pent up emotions. Maybe a few dummies of trade union leaders in Britain could do a great deal to relieve industrial unrest and end strikes!

*

Meteorologists selected the date of Queen Elizabeth II's Coronation as 2 June 1953, because it was said to be the day when there was consistently no rain. It rained.

*

The distance between the wingtips of a Boeing 747 is longer than the first flight made by the Wright Brothers.

Coin operated slot machines were first invented in around 100 BC to dispense holy water to monks and priests.

*

Laughing gas, or nitrous oxide, was discovered in 1800 and was used at parties for giving people 'a trip'. People found that it made them 'high' and they felt very elated.

*

While examining urine, during an experiment to find the philosopher's stone, German chemist Henning Brand discovered phosphorous.

*

A tailor named Teichelt in 1911 invented a batwing cape that would allow him to fly from the top of the Eiffel Tower. Crowds gathered to watch his first flight on a cold December morning. He leapt from the first level of the Tower and . . . splat! End of experiment and the end of Teichelt.

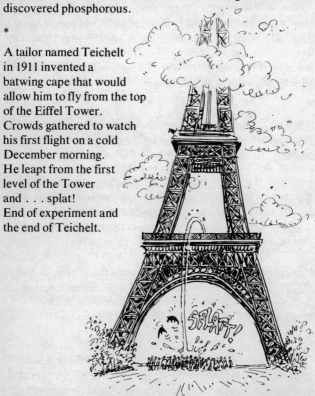

Benjamin Franklin was the first to invent bi-focal glasses.
Fed-up with wearing two different pairs, he chopped the
lenses in half, and put half of each in one pair of frames. It
worked!

*

The company Proctor and Gamble were the first to patent a
baby's nappy that let the mother know when it needed
changing. It inflated when the baby urinated. Surprisingly the
idea hasn't caught on!

*

One of the few successful inventions produced purely for
financial reward was the safety pin. In 1849, Walter Hunt was
heavily in debt so he sat down one afternoon with the
intention of inventing a money-making product. Three hours
later he had created the safety-pin.

*

The first warm toilet seat was the invention of Mr George
Rhodes, secretary of the Society of Inventors in Manchester,
England.

*

Bubble gum was invented in 1928 by one Walter Diemer, who
was told that it was a crazy idea and it would never catch on.
Today it is a 150-million-dollar a year business.

*

Having invented the light-bulb, Thomas Edison found that
they could be put to some very interesting and practical uses,
not only was a light-bulb put on the end of a conductor's
baton, but also on the busts of Broadway dancers!

*

The first water closet was invented by Queen Elizabeth I's
godson. She tried it out at his home and immediately decided
to have one installed in her palace. The royal throne room?

Unbelievable though it may sound – the cigarette lighter was invented before the match. J. W. Dobereiner in 1816 found a way of automatically igniting a jet of hydrogen, and the cigarette lighter was born.

*

In 1860 an American inventor invented a piano with a curved keyboard. Why? For players with short arms, of course!

Undoubtedly one of the greatest inventions must be the telephone, a lifeline for many. Unfortunately nothing is infallible. The worst wrong number on record is that of a BBC employee who attempted to ring a local number in Walthamstow and got . . . the laundry room of the Empire State Building in New York!

*

The ultimate in anti-theft devices must surely be the Kim-Protege, invented by Emile Kimmerle. It is triggered off when a thief touches a trip wire, this causes tear gas to be sprayed at him, at the same time knockout gas falls from the ceiling, ankle grips shoot out and grab his legs, and finally he is sprayed with red sticky labels that say THIEF. Not many could escape from that!

*

The most efficient form of light production discovered so far is the glow-worm.

*

The goose-step was an invention of the British, not the Germans as is popularly believed.

*

Chou Kung, inventor of the compass, had a hand which could swivel in a complete circle on the end of his wrist.

*

For a number of years the Aurélien School published a rubber newspaper for naked people. The newspaper could be read in the bath without going soggy.

Jokers Wild

'Wit is a treacherous dart.
It is perhaps the only weapon with
which it is possible to stab
oneself in one's own back.'

Geoffrey Bocca

One of the cleverest wartime jokes played on Axis agents was when Field Marshal Montgomery visited North Africa in a much publicised trip. This kept the Nazis occupied, but what they didn't know was that it was a Montgomery 'look-alike'. Whilst an eye was kept on the actor posing as the Field Marshal, the real 'Monty' was planning an invasion of Nazi-held Europe.

*

The first mermaid to be spotted was off the coast of Cornwall in 1825. It appeared at moonlight and sat on a rock, singing as it preened itself in a mirror. This phenomenon appeared several nights in succession and drew large crowds, until it finally burst into a chorus of *God Save The King* and sank slowly into the sea, never to appear again. In reality it was a clergyman in drag! The Reverend Robert Hawker set out to test the power of the mermaid myth, and certainly succeeded in proving that it was just that . . . a myth.

*

Practical joker, King Edward VII, when still Prince of Wales – which was most of his life – was a great friend of the actress Sarah Bernhardt. In one of her dramatic productions she was on stage in the corpse scene of *Fedora*, weeping over the corpse of her murdered lover when she looked down and saw that the 'corpse' was none other than the Prince of Wales!

*

The Thracians had a philosophy that when a person died he or she went to a much happier place and left behind all the misery of the earth. Instead of crying at a death, the Thracians naturally burst out laughing, and always joked on behalf of the departed who they assumed was now having the 'time of his life'!

Kings and Queens

'Those who see and observe kings, heroes, and statesmen, discover that they have headaches, indigestion, humours and passions, just like other people; every one of which in their turn determine their wills in defiance of their reason.'

Lord Chesterfield

When Captain Cook landed on the island of Tonga during his third voyage of 1777 he met the octogenarian King Lapetemaka II. During their conversations the king told Cook that it was his duty to deflower every native virgin. He claimed that he had never been to bed with the same woman twice and proudly told his visitor that he was still performing the regal duty between eight and ten times a day.

*

During his reign Charles II 'touched' almost 100,000 sufferers from scrofula who hoped to be cured by the royal hand.

*

King Abdul Aziz Ibn Saud of Saudi Arabia, between 1932 and 1953, had 300 wives.

*

King George II of England had an unfortunate death. He was the only monarch of England to fall off a toilet seat.

*

The longest reign in Egypt is the ninety-year one of Pepi II, who must have succeeded to the throne at an extremely early age. When he died Egypt practically collapsed.

*

In twenty-two years between 1605 and 1627, Jahangir, the fourth Mogul Emperor, had a harem of 300 wives, 5000 mistresses and 1000 young men for alternative sexual pleasures.

*

In 1819 King John IV of Portugal acquired the first royal hearing aid. A large throne with openings in the hollow arms which visitors spoke into, their voices being channelled into a flexible pipe which the King held to his ear.

Mary, Queen of Scots, had a watch shaped like a human skull.

*

The latest recorded coronation after succession is thirty-five years *after death*. Czar Peter III was assassinated in 1762, and it was not until 1797 that the king was removed from his coffin and was officially crowned.

*

A common belief is that royal blood should never be allowed to spill on the ground. As a result some of the most unusual forms of assassination have taken place. In 1688 the King of Siam had a relation placed in a large mortar and had him pounded to death with a pestle. The blood was all contained in the vessel and not one drop spilled on the ground.

*

King Richard III and Louis XIV were born with teeth.

*

King Henry I of England declared that a yard should be thirty-six inches, this was because his arm happened to be this length. If his arm had been thirty inches or even twenty-eight inches, this is how long a yard would have been, and consequently a 'foot' would not have been twelve inches. Perhaps if his arm had been thirty inches long we would have gone metric in the twelfth century!

*

Queen Marie Antoinette and King Louis XIV of France might have escaped execution had it not been for a twist of fate in 1791. Whilst attempting to escape from France the horses of their coach had to be changed. Deciding that they would get out of the coach to wait whilst the horses were changed, the King and Queen were recognised and began their journey to the next world. Had they remained inside the coach, they would have escaped. If it had been raining, for instance, maybe Marie Antoinette would not have lost her pretty head.

Frederick the Great used to have his veins opened in battle to calm his nerves.

*

In 1167 King Charles VII of Sweden was executed. What happened to King Charles I, II, III, IV, V and VI, did they follow the same fate? No, they didn't exist. Charles VII was the first king to take the name Charles, but why the VII nobody knows.

*

William III, Queen Anne, George I, George II, George III and George IV all died on Saturdays.

*

Attila the Hun was a dwarf.

King Alfonso of Spain was tone deaf. He employed a man with one important duty – that of standing up when the National Anthem was played so that the King could recognise the tune.

*

The greatest number of weather forecasters ever employed by one monarch at any one time was 5000. This was Kublai Khan. Their numbers quickly decreased because if they made a mistake about the weather they forfeited their heads.

*

Maurice, Count of Saxony, once bent a nail into the shape of a corkscrew with his fingers and used it to open a bottle of wine.

*

The most expensive robe ever worn belonged to Louis XIV. It was encrusted with diamonds and cost one-sixth of the value of the Palace of Versailles.

*

In mourning for her beloved husband, Queen Victoria ordered that his clothes be laid out on his bed every day . . . for forty years.

*

Queen Austrichilda in 580 AD when she became ill demanded that if she died her doctors would too. Trying desperately hard to keep her alive for their own sakes, the doctors unfortunately failed and were executed.

*

Probably one of the strongest monarchs was King Edward III. The sword he used took two ordinary men to lift.

The Queen with the largest wardrobe was Elizabeth I of Russia. She used to change her clothes on average twelve times a day and on her death some 15,000 dresses were discovered in her possession.

*

The first time a monarch was given chloroform to ease the pains of childbirth was in 1853. Until this time clergymen had condemned the use of chloroform believing that 'in sorrow' a woman should bring forth children. Nothing more was said about it after 1853 . . .

*

When George I became King of England in 1714 his wife did not become Queen because she had committed adultery.

*

The most expensive coronation robes in the world were worn by Emperor Bokassa of the Central African Empire at his crowning in 1977. The robes cost £77,000, his country being noted as the poorest in Africa.

*

King Saul is the first recorded person to have committed suicide by falling on his sword.

*

In history it is believed that kings and queens should die standing up, and Queen Elizabeth I is said to have stood for two days waiting to die, expiring at the last uttering those immortal words: 'All my possessions for a moment in time.'

Love Conquers All

'Love is one damned fool after another.'

Anon.

People from the Philippines have a unique way of kissing – they put their lips to each other's face and inhale very quickly.

*

World champion kissers are Paul Trevillion and Sadie Nine, who in 1975 achieved the record of 20,009 kisses in two hours. After training Sadie managed to double the size of her lips.

*

The first International Conference of Love and Attraction was held in 1977. It came to the conclusion that love is now dying out and that permissive sex has taken its place.

*

Lucrezia Borgia was married four times before she was twenty-two.

*

Democritus is said to have blinded himself because he could not look at a woman without wanting to have sex with her.

*

The most unusual wedding on record is that of Arturo Santora and Barbara Durante, who married *on the bottom of the sea* in San Frutosis Bay. Everyone involved in the ceremony, including the bride, wore deep-sea diving gear and breathing apparatus. The bride's bouquet was made of coral.

*

The actress Sarah Bernhardt had over 1000 lovers during her life, and the rosewood coffin she slept in was lined with their love letters.

*

The marriage of Louis XIV and Marie Antoinette was not consummated until seven years after their wedding.

*

The USSR was the first country to legalise abortion, in 1920.

Howard Hughes once wrote four pages of notes about Jane Russell's bosom.

*

A 1970 census in the USA revealed that 2983 men were widowers at the age of *fourteen*! Nearly 300 women of the same age were either widowed or divorced.

*

After Sir Walter Raleigh was executed in 1618, his widow had his head embalmed and kept it in a red leather bag which she carried everywhere until her own death twenty-nine years later.

*

By a law of King Canute, a woman convicted of adultery forfeited 'both nose and ears'.

*

There have been several recorded cases of eunuchs who have remained sexually competent and in one instance the castrate was married for nine years and led a perfectly normal sex life.

*

An eighty-eight-year-old Iranian man attributed his sexual powers to eating two pounds of raw onions every day, (onions were considered an aphrodisiac) and to prove its success rate he married 168 times.

*

The longest screen kiss occurred in the 1941 film *You're in the Army Now*, when Regis Toomey and Jane Wyman held a kiss for over three minutes.

*

The most popular misconception is that men's fancy turns to love in the spring. This is not really true, for male sex hormones are at their peak in autumn and winter. Whether or not this is because the temperatures are lower and male sperms are more active in the cold is not known.

*

Casanova, one of the world's greatest lovers, maintained that he encountered more licentiousness in England than in any other country he visited. He boasted that he always used British contraceptives, which experience had taught him to be the best.

Men always like a woman who has that little 'something extra', and Henry VIII's second wife Anne Boleyn certainly had more than most – not only did she have an extra finger on her left hand, but she also had three breasts.

The French novelist, Nicholas Restif de la Bretonne had read much by the age of four, was said to have seduced girls by the time he was eleven and at fourteen he wrote a poem based on his first twelve mistresses, making him one of the youngest 'Casanova's' in the world.

*

It is believed that all animals have a particular scent that makes them attractive to members of the opposite sex. Women are said to have a destinct sexual aroma that attracts men to them, although it is not consciously apparent. With animals, however, this is a totally different matter. The male emperor moth can smell a virgin female of the same species 11 km (6.8 miles) away, upwind.

*

Prunes used to be served as free lunches in Elizabethan brothels.

*

On 14 May, 1939 Lina Medina gave birth to a healthy, bouncing baby in Lima, Peru. The mother was aged five years eight months at the time.

Male of the Species

'A man in the house is worth two in the street.'

Mae West

Before 600 BC all Greek and Roman statues of naked men showed them to have testicles of equal size. After this time the left testicle was always larger and lower than the right.

*

In one single orgasm three hundred million sperm are ejaculated from a pulsating male penis. Only one needs to make the journey of twelve centimetres to the ovum.

*

There is no truth in the belief that men react more to erotic visual stimuli than women, despite the fact that newspapers and magazines frequently portray naked women, whilst erotica of males exposing their genitals is rarely found.

Many tests have been made over the centuries to test whether or not acquired physical characteristics can be inherited. They can't, of course, otherwise Jewish babies would by now not be born with a fully developed foreskin.

Men's blood is richer in red blood cells than that of women, containing more than two million red blood cells more per cubic centimetre.

*

Castration is the only proven means of preventing baldness in men.

*

The size of a man bears no relation to the size of his penis. A manual worker 180 cm (5ft 11 in) tall, weighing 92 kg (200 lb) may have a much smaller penis than a bank clerk 150 cm (4ft 8 in) tall, weighing 55 kg (120 lb).

*

The size of a man's penis in an unstimulated state will have no relation to its length when erect. A penis measuring 7.5 cm (3 in) when flaccid will be doubled to 15 cm (6 in) when erect, but the man whose penis measures 11 cm (4½ in) will reach 16 cm (6¼ in) when erect, an increase of just 5 cm (2 in). Either way, the size of a man's penis makes no difference to his abilities as a lover.

*

The condition known as 'blue balls' (when men believe that their testicles ache because of infrequent sex) is a psychological condition only.

*

Men under thirty have the ability to reach orgasm again within five minutes of an ejaculation. Men who are over fifty usually only ejaculate once in twenty-four hours.

*

Baby boys frequently have erections. The first erection may occur immediately after birth.

Male spermatozoa are produced in man's testicles at the rate of 50,000 every minute.

*

During ejaculation the seminal fluid of a normal healthy male may spurt a distance of 50 cm (20 in).

*

Ten million vasectomy operations are performed every year.

*

In Asia the most powerful aphrodisiac and cure for impotence is powdered rhinoceros horn. The rhinoceros horn resembles an erect penis – which might have something to do with it!

*

One of the greatest dilemmas faced by artists for hunderds of years was whether Adam had a navel or not.

*

The average man working in a mild climate loses 2.83 litres (5 pts) of fluid in the form of sweat every day. A miner may lose up to 6.15 litres (13 pints) per shift and an Indian working in the sun up to 11.35 litres (20 pts) per day.

*

Ten times as many men as women are colour blind. Most of them have difficulty with the colour green.

*

The largest erect penis on record measured fourteen inches.

*

During his ten-year research for his revealing study *Sexual Behaviour and the Human Male* Alfred Kinsey cited the case of one man who had averaged 33.1 acts of sex every week over a period of thirty years! This total averaged a rate of more than five sexual encounters a day and the grand total fell not far short of 52,000. (Kinsey's study indicated that the mean frequency for the average man was a paltry 2.3 acts a week.)

*

Research into a contraceptive pill for men quickly produced an effective result. Unfortunately users of the pill found that their eyeballs turned red when they drank alcohol. The research began again.

*

The male population of France are so exhausted after their weekends that only five per cent have enough energy left to make love on Mondays.

*

The weight of male babies at birth range quite considerably from just under 2 lb (the lightest) to 29 lb (the heaviest). There is a much greater chance of survival if babies are born weighing around an average 7 lb 4 oz.

*

Every year in Britain approximately 91,500 men undergo some kind of surgery on their genital organs.

*

The smallest recorded normal functioning penis measured just under half an inch in length.

*

Apart from variations in size, men imagine that all penises are physically the same. This is not true. There are three different types of penis, the blunt type, the bottle type, and the prow type. These are the names given to the variations in shape of the head of the penis. All men have one of these three shapes, but the variations are insignificant, are only obvious on close examination, and make no difference whatsoever to the function or arousal of the penis.

If the tubes inside the testicles which carry the sperm to the penis were uncoiled they would stretch a distance of more than twenty feet.

*

The normal healthy adult male's testicles produce thirty billion sperm a month. If they are not 'used' they simply pass out in the urine unnoticed.

*

The fastest erection recorded (from flaccid to fully erect) is three seconds.

*

The lowest number of orgasms recorded is one ejaculation in thirty years.

*

The greatest number of multiple ejaculations on record is eight separate ejaculations in one hour.

*

In normal semen seventy-five per cent of the sperm move at a rate of three millimetres a minute.

*

The earliest known orgasm for a boy is five months. There is no ejaculation because this is physically impossible at such an early age.

*

Only three men in every 1000 are physically capable of sucking their own penis.

*

Only five men in every thousand can achieve orgasm through fantasy alone with no physical contact of any kind.

Among primates and carnivores, men and hyenas are the only animals not to have a penis bone. Monkeys, apes, dolphins, cats, dogs, and even rats and mice have a bone in the penis. This is also true for the female of the species, with the human female not having a clitoris bone.

*

Japanese men, when speaking, bow to each other on average 2000 times a day. The depth of bow is subtly calculated, the lower or inferior person bowing lower than his superior.

Numbers and Vital Statistics

'One has to be able to count if only so that
at fifty one doesn't marry a girl of twenty.'

Maxim Gorky

In March 1890, 180,000 mummified cats were auctioned in Liverpool. They were sold by the ton for fertiliser. Just one of the many uses of a dead cat!

*

The highest price in history for a television advertisement was for the Super Bowl in 1978, which cost over £175,000 a minute.

*

To obtain one ounce of gold miners have dug as deep as two and a half miles.

*

Since the advent of electricity the average American now sleeps one and a half hours less each night.

*

The Hermitage Art Gallery in Russia is the largest in the world with more than three million works of art. Visitors who walk around all the treasures rarely realise that in doing so they have walked a distance of fifteen miles.

*

During the two year period when the Mona Lisa was stolen, 1911-1913, six Americans individually paid 300,000 dollars for what they believed was the original.

*

The people of the United States make on average 350,000,000 telephone calls every day.

*

In 1976 banknotes to the value of 2000 DM fluttered out of the sky over Limburg in Germany. They were picked up by two clergymen.

The Mona Lisa is now the most valuable painting in the world, and is insured for a mere fifty million pounds.

*

Any married couple going for an eleven day honeymoon have around one million seconds in which to enjoy themselves.

*

To count to one million would take a long time, but it sounds perfectly feasible for one person to do it – in fact a fifty-one-year-old housewife, Mrs Marva Drew, typed out the numbers one to a million. It took five years and 2473 sheets of paper – but how long would it take to count a billion? If you assume that a person is able to count to 200 in one minute, that he is allowed twelve hours' rest a day and that he is endowed with immortality, he would need 19,024 years, 68 days, 10 hours and 40 minutes to count to one billion.

A normal healthy adult gives off the same amount of heat as a 120-watt bulb, which is why a room full of people can get pretty hot.

*

Odour technicians who work in perfume factories have such sensitive noses that they can distinguish between 20,000 different odours.

*

On a hot day an oak tree gives off 28,000 gallons of moisture.

*

A single drop of water is made up of 1,700,000,000,000,000,000 molecules. If a single drop of water was magnified to the size of the world, each molecule would be the size of an orange.

*

Bamboo grows faster than any other plant and in just twenty-four hours may grow more than a metre.

*

The giant sequoia tree is the longest living tree known to man and can live forever. They take 200 years to reach sexual maturity, after which time it bears millions of tiny seeds.

*

Milan Cathedral took 579 years to build.

*

The earth travels more than 2,413,950 km (1½ million miles) every day.

*

In *One Hundred Days of Sodom* the Marquis de Sade catalogued 600 different ways of making love.

The word 'girl' appears in the Bible only once.

*

Half a billion people – about one person in eight – are suffering from chronic malnutrition in the world today.

*

A kitchen erected to cope with serious famine in India served 1,200,000 meals a day in April 1973.

*

The wrinkled grey covering of the human brain is made up of 9,000,000,000 cells.

*

In twenty-four hours the average healthy adult breathes 23,000 times, eats about 1.36 kg (3 lbs) of food and drinks approximately 1.18 litres (2½ pints) of liquid. In that time his hair grows 0.43535 mm (0.01714 ins) and his nails 0.00116 mm (0.00004 ins).

*

In the next sixty seconds 100 people will die.

*

In 1972 the defence budget of Andorra was the equivalent of £2.00.

*

In AD 193 the World was auctioned and was bought by a Roman senator for £19½ million. Unfortunately he died sixty-six days later.

*

Dogs in New York excrete 175 tons of faecal matter on to the streets every day. In 1978 a 'Pooper-scooper' law was passed that orders dog owners to make amends if their dogs foul the pavements, and are fined if their dog leaves a deposit behind!

To produce the paper on which one Sunday edition of the *New York Times* is printed requires 63,000 trees.

*

In the USA seven million cars go to the scrapyards annually.

*

30,000 tonnes of cosmic dust are deposited on the earth every year.

*

It is estimated that there are eighty million people in the world with the surname 'Chang'.

*

The human body contains enough phosphorous to make the heads of 2000 matches, enough fat for seven bars of soap and enough iron to make one nail.

*

Agony column writer, Marjorie Proops, receives on average 30,000 letters a year from people requesting her help.

*

The Department of Health list approximately 1000 different surgical operations that can be performed on the human body.

Out of this World

'The Cosmos is a gigantic flywheel making
10,000 revolutions a minute.
Man is a sick fly taking a dizzy ride on it.
Religion is the theory that the wheel was designed
and set spinning to give him a ride.'

H. L. Mencken

There are 4000 items of space research instruments and their assorted debris littering outer space.

*

The hottest part of the sun is over 20,000,000°C.

*

The most beautiful sight in the universe is said to be a urine dump out in space. Well, even spacemen have to go! It is released through a nozzle in the space ship and as it is released into space it bursts into ten million ice crystals like a sparkler in outer space, and shoots off in all directions in a most spectacular manner.

*

The volume of the sun is more than one million earths put together.

*

A lightning bolt is five times hotter than the surface of the sun.

*

The Arend-Roland comet which orbits the earth every 10,000 years was first sighted in 1957.

*

The heaviest meteorite that has fallen on the earth weighs an estimated sixty tons, although it has never been moved and can still be seen in Africa where it landed.

*

Modern telescopes enable us to look at galaxies 4000 million miles away.

*

In the afternoon the temperature on Mars is 80°F.

*

Uranus takes eighty-four years to orbit the sun.

The sun burns 240,000,000 tons of hydrogen dust every minute.

*

Not one science fiction writer anticipated that there would be craters on the planet Mars.

*

In the last 600 million years some 2000 asteroids have collided with the earth, but have not knocked it out of orbit.

*

To set out on a direct flight from earth to the planet Pluto on the edge of the solar system would take forty-seven years.

*

After a forest fire in Alaska in 1950 when sulphur particles entered the atmosphere on the night of 26 September of that year there was a *blue moon*.

*

The oldest moon rock yet brought back to earth is estimated to be 4720 million years old.

*

Every year it takes the moon just slightly longer to encircle the earth than it did the year before – two-thousandth of a second longer – because it is gradually moving away from the earth. The sun will have burned itself out by the time the moon moves much further away than its present distance, which will be in five billion years time when the earth will certainly cease to exist.

*

Comets appear in regular cycles, Halley's Comet being the oldest recorded comet, having first been spotted in 467 BC and every seventy-five years since (its next appearance will be at approximately 9.30 pm on 9 February, 1986). The most extreme comet must be Delevan's Comet which was seen in 1914 and will not return for another 24,000,000 years.

*

If the entire solar system were scaled down so that the sun was the size of a ball approximately one foot in diameter, in the same proportions the nearest star would still be 5500 miles away.

*

Andromeda is the remotest object in the universe visible to the naked eye. It is 13,000,000,000,000,000,000 miles away.

Power Mad

'Power can corrupt, but absolute power
is absolutely delightful.'

Anon.

The greatest tyrant in the history of mankind is said to be the Ming Emperor Hung Wu (1368-98) who would have anybody who displeased him in anyway whatsoever executed on the spot. His tyranny got so bad towards the end of his reign that every person associated with him before setting out to see him would say farewell to their families just in case they did not return.

*

Napoleon Bonaparte suffered from ailurophobia –
a terror of cats.

*

Scanderburg, a fifteenth century king of Albania, once executed two prisoners bound together by cutting them in half at the waist, with one blow from his sword.

*

Emperor Justinian II in 695 AD had his nose cut off by the power-mad Leontius, leader of a rebellious group in Constantinople, in an attempt to topple him from power. In 698 AD General Tiberius III became Emperor and believing in an 'eye for an eye, and a tooth for a tooth' he had Leontius' nose cut off in revenge. Revenge is sweet, and Justinian returned and killed both Leontius and Tiberius and resumed his former position as Emperor!

In 1860 some 400,000 households in Southern America owned black slaves.

*

In 604 AD the Caliph of Omar ordered the destruction of the famous library at Alexandria. The books were used to heat the city baths and are said to have provided enough fuel to keep the baths heated for more than six months.

*

During the American Revolution boys as young as twelve years old could be thrown into jail by Army Officers if they refused to perform any tasks requested of them.

*

Leonardo da Vinci could break a horseshoe with his bare hands.

*

King Philip of France declared any kind of skin disease a punishable offence, and many people suffering from leprosy were put to death.

*

Ismail the bloodthirsty, sometime ruler of Morocco, is reputed to have fathered 548 sons and 340 daughters.

Quick and the Dead

'Henry's the sort that keeps
you guessing as to whether
he's going to deliver a speech,
or wet the bed.'

(Said of Henry Wallace)

According to Rasputin's lovers, his penis measured 'a good thirteen inches when fully erect'.

*

Dr Ashley Clarke of Leicester University, England, in 1979 was awarded the title of the 'Most Boring Lecturer' after giving a dissertation on the 'classical mechanical formulation for motion in an infinite viscous medium'.

*

Before going before a firing squad, world famous spy Mata Hari had a new suit especially made to die in.

*

The word 'Eureka!' is always associated with Archimedes and is frequently accompanied in our mind's eye with a mental picture of him leaping completely naked out of his bath and running through the streets. This might cause a sensation today, but in Ancient Greece everyone exercised naked, and the sight of a nude man was so common that the people in the street would not have batted an eyelid.

*

The artist Picasso lived for seven years with Fernande Olivier, a woman separated from her husband. Not knowing where he was she was unable to obtain a divorce and so the two were unable to marry. Some forty years later she discovered by chance that her husband had died on the very day she had met Picasso.

*

Leonard Henriksson, a Swedish film cameraman, was murdered in Chile. Filming at the time, he actually filmed close-up pictures of the men as they shot and killed him, making him the only person in the world to film his own killers.

Albert Einstein was a very late developer and was unable to speak until he was nine years old.

*

Mac Norton, known professionally as the *Human Aquarium*, once swallowed three gallons of water and two dozen live frogs in one go.

*

Napoleon's 2.54 cm (1 in) long penis was offered for auction at Christie's in 1972 but failed to reach the reserve price.

*

Walter Monckton worked for King Edward VIII (later Duke of Windsor) voluntarily for twenty-five years. His reward at the end was a cigarette case with his name spelt incorrectly.

*

Abraham Lincoln thought all his life that he was illegitimate and claimed that bastards are far more intelligent than other people. After his assassination it was discovered that he was legitimate.

*

In 1912 Theodore Roosevelt was shot in the chest whilst making a speech. He finished his speech before having any medical attention.

*

Dr Samuel Johnson once drank thirty-six glasses of port in one evening without getting up from his seat the whole time. Quite a record!

*

William Buckland, nineteenth century Dean of Westminster, ate Louis XIV's embalmed heart for dinner one evening.

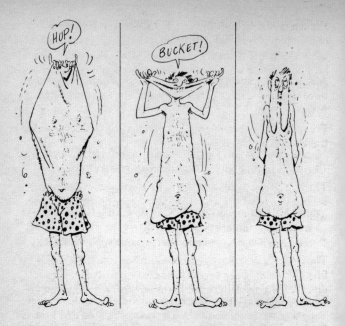

John Morris had 'elastic skin' and could pull the skin of his chest up over his head and his cheeks out more than eight inches from the side of his face.

*

Sir Isaac Newton was a member of parliament, but his only recorded speech is when he made a request for the windows to be opened as it was getting hot.

*

Mathematician and astrologer Girolamo Cardano predicted the day on which he was going to die – 21 September, 1576 – but when he woke up on that day in perfect health and there seemed little chance of dying he committed suicide.

French minister for finance, Jacques Necker, created a unique tomb for the wife he loved – he had her placed in a basin of alcohol so that he could look at her every day. When he died his body was placed alongside hers and the tomb was closed.

*

Freud could never comprehend a railway timetable, so never travelled alone.

*

The first Prime Minister to be born in a Ladies' Cloakroom was Sir Winston Churchill. His mother gave birth prematurely whilst at a dance.

*

The longest delay on record for awarding a Nobel Prize is fifty-five years in the case of Francis Peyton Rous, who discovered a strain of cancer virus in 1910 and was given the Prize in 1966 when he was 87 years old.

*

The vainest man recorded was Archduke Ferdinand of Austria who was sewn into his uniforms so that they didn't look creased. This led to his death because when he was shot in 1914 it was impossible to undo his uniform. He bled to death.

*

Annette Kellerman in 1909 became the first woman to be arrested for indecent exposure. She was wearing a bathing suit that had short sleeves and trousers that only came down as far as her knees. Shocking!

*

Assassins burst into Leon Trotsky's bedroom and aimed over seventy bullets at the bed. Trotsky escaped unhurt, possibly one of the luckiest escapes on record.

Stuntman Bobby Leech made a daring plunge over the Niagara Falls in a barrel, breaking practically every bone in his body – but lived to tell the tale. He died several years later . . . he slipped on a banana skin.

*

German strongman Siegmund Brettbart was able to bite through 5 mm thick steel bars, break chains by expanding his chest, and could push large nails through iron with his bare fist.

*

A French actor named Pierre Messie could make his hair stand on end at will.

*

Arnold Bennett, author of *The Old Wives' Tale*, died of typhoid in Paris in 1931 after drinking a glass of water to prove that the local water was perfectly safe to drink.

Remarkable Talent

'It took me fifteen years to discover I had no talent for writing, but I couldn't give it up because by that time I was too famous.'

Robert Benchley

A close examination of Grimm's fairy tales reveals that the brothers could be accused of being sexist, for the stories are packed with wicked stepmothers, evil witches, bloodthirsty young maidens and women who kill their lovers. Out of some 200 stories there are only three wicked fathers, two wizards and one man who kills, but more than sixty evil ladies.

*

Artist Pablo Picasso very nearly did not get an opportunity to use his talents. At birth the midwife thought he was stillborn and put him to one side ready to be disposed of. Fortunately he revived.

*

The atomic bomb first appeared in a novel by H. G. Wells in 1914 called *The World Set Free*.

*

America's most prolific songwriter, Irving Berlin, never learnt to read or write music. He dictated everything that came into his head.

*

The greatest forger of art was Hans Van Meegeren who was skilled at producing 'genuine' Vermeers, many of which he sold for vast sums. His downfall came when he sold one to the Nazi leader, Hermann Göring. Accused of collaboration after the war, he admitted his forgeries and so opted for prison rather than the death penalty.

*

Edgar Allen Poe wrote most of his mystery and horror stories under the influence of opium and alcohol.

*

During his lifetime Van Gogh sold only one painting.

'Positively harmful to the mind . . . unsuitable for children . . .' These remarks were made about one of the great literary masterpieces for children – Hans Christian Andersen's *Fairy Tales* – when first published.

*

One of the most controversial twentieth century writers, D. H. Lawrence, author of *Lady Chatterley's Lover*, enjoyed climbing mulberry trees, completely naked.

*

Harry Houdini once remained submerged in a sealed metal coffin for 1 hour 42 minutes. Before he successfully resurfaced it was estimated that the air supply was only sufficient to last fifteen minutes.

*

A stamp was issued in Albania in honour of Ahmed Zogu I who had achieved the dubious distinction of smoking 240 cigarettes a day.

Best selling author, Harriet Beecher Stowe, received hate mail after the publication of *Uncle Tom's Cabin*. Inside one letter was a human ear.

*

La Morte d'Arthur, a now classic work, was written whilst the author, Sir Thomas Malory, was serving a prison sentence for rape.

*

Percy Bysshe Shelley had a remarkably small head.

*

The highest sales of a paperback work of fiction is 4,253,500 copies of D. H. Lawrence's *Lady Chatterley's Lover*.

*

The shortest review on record came from Brian Brennan, book and TV critic, whose review of the American TV serial *Soap* published on 1 December, 1979, consisted of one word: 'WOW!'

Socrates and Homer are considered by most to be the two greatest figures in the history of literature, yet not one word of their writings actually exists.

*

Pope Paul IV was so shocked by the sight of naked figures in Michaelangelo's 'Last Judgement' that he commissioned another artist to paint clothes on them!

*

Legendary markswoman, Annie Oakley, once shot the ash from the end of a cigarette that Crown Prince William of Germany was holding between his lips. She fired from a range of 30.48 m (100 ft).

Sporting Chance

'The only athletic sport I ever
mastered was backgammon.'

Douglas Jerrold

Legless swimmer Guy Noel holds an endurance record for swimming two hundred hours in a French canal.

*

During the winter months the horsemen of northern Afghanistan play a wild form of polo using a headless calf as the ball. This unique game is called 'buz khashi'.

*

'Water Sports' is the name given to a sexual activity favoured by a small percentage of the population in which each partner drinks the urine of the other. Having drunk a lot of liquid a long session of water sports can be maintained by recycling the fluid from one body to another. This is not a harmful practice, unless pathogenic bacteria are present in the urine, but it is purely a matter of taste!

*

In 1905 nineteen boys died during rough games of soccer at school, the greatest number of footballers to die as a result of the game in one year.

*

The most popular sport in the United States is golf and there are more than 10,000 golf courses in the country to prove it.

*

Making love uses half as many calories as skipping.

*

Philippine basketball players can be fined up to 150 dollars for spitting at the referee.

*

During a football game in Argentina in 1972 a linesman was kicked to death by the players for his decision. The entire team were arrested and put into prison.

*

The most popular sport in American nudist camps is volleyball.

That's Entertainment

'If she were cast as Lady Godiva
the horse would steal the act.'

(Of a certain actress)

Eighteenth century French actor Jean Marie Collot d'Herbois was such a bad actor that during a performance at Lyons he was actually booed off stage. Taking up another profession, he later returned as a Justice of the Peace during the French Revolution and ordered the death of 6000 Lyons citizens. Revenge is sweet.

*

Theatrical performances by companies of young boys were so popular in the sixteenth century that Shakespeare refers to them in *Hamlet* as posing a considerable threat to professional adult actors.

*

One of the most famous songs from any film musical must surely be Gene Kelly's *Singing in the Rain*, but although it is his voice singing the song, the squelchy tap dancing in the puddles heard on the recording are not the sound of Mr Kelly's feet but two girls dancing in a bucket of water which was dubbed onto the film afterwards!

The actress Shirley Temple made over one million dollars before she was ten years old.

*

In his first twenty-nine films, Humphrey Bogart was electrocuted or hanged in eight, shot in twelve, and was a jailbird in nine of them.

*

The 1933 King Kong was a hand puppet 15.24 cms (6 ins) high.

*

George Balanchine choreographed a ballet for elephants with music by Stravinsky. Truly the *greatest* show on earth!

*

The actor Peter Finch was the only person to win an Oscar posthumously.

*

Fred Astaire's legs were insured for 650,000 dollars.

*

The legendary Italian film star Maciste could open a tin of sardines by squeezing it with his fingers.

*

Horror movie stars Peter Cushing, Vincent Price and Christopher Lee were all born on 27 May.

*

The first copyrighted motion picture in the United States was a film of a man sneezing.

During a performance of the play *Little Dragon* in Taiwan an actress actually gave birth on stage. The audience all thought it was part of the play and no doubt considered it to be an award-winning performance.

*

The first big Broadway hit musical of Rogers and Hammerstein was *Oklahoma!* for which Richard Rogers wrote the entire musical score in just five hours.

*

In 1940 Tommy Dorsey and his band gave a concert to the monkeys of Philadelphia Zoo. The audience's response was described by a zoo official as 'negative'.

*

The 1890 film *Histoire d'un Crime* was the first film in which the flashback technique was used, when a murderer dreamt of his heinous crimes.

*

The sex film industry's equivalent of an Oscar is a statuette of a naked female known as the Erotica.

Under Doctor's Orders

'Your body is the baggage you must
carry through life. The more excess baggage,
the shorter the trip.'

Arnold H. Glasgow

Doctor's records prove that people who smoke filter-tipped cigarettes are in danger of dying four years earlier than those who smoke filterless cigarettes. Higher levels of carbon monoxide enter the body because a filter prevents oxygen diluting the smoke. Death will be through lung cancer or cardiac arrest in sixty per cent of cases.

*

The anaesthetic effects of ether were discovered by an American chemistry student who had observed the effects of gas on young people who sniffed it at parties.

*

Munchhausen Syndrome is the name given to the 'mental' condition of bogus patients, people addicted to hospital who will voluntarily undergo unnecessary operations, and deliberately inflict wounds upon themselves or swallow foreign bodies just to get into hospital. The worst recorded case of Munchhausen Syndrome is that of a six-year-old British girl who caused herself to enter hospital some twelve times, had seven major X-rays, six examinations under anaesthetic, had her urine analysed 150 times, and underwent numerous unnecessary and painful courses of treatment. All the time she was in perfect health.

*

Women in Egypt have been known to lie face upwards under a passing train as a remedy for sterility. Others have lain face downwards to prevent a pregnancy.

*

Leonardo da Vinci, when studying human anatomy, was accused of dissecting the bodies of people who were still alive.

*

In Japanese hospitals there are no wards numbered four or nine. The reason? The Japanese word 'four' is similar in sound to the word 'death' and 'nine' sounds like the word for 'suffering'. Because of the psychological effect it might have on a patient to discover that he or she is in 'death ward', the numbers are tactfully avoided.

*

Between 1618-48 a smallpox epidemic in Europe caused the deaths of sixty million people.

*

The most complex matter in the entire Universe is still the human brain.

*

Anyone with 'flu can usually sneeze at a velocity of 103 miles an hour, sending approximately 85,000,000 'flu viruses (per sneeze) a distance of twelve feet, which is why it is very easy to catch!

*

In the 1830's tomato ketchup was patented for the first time as a medicine in America.

*

Cholera bacteria will increase in size sixteen million times in twelve hours in the right conditions.

*

Hospital related infections are on the increase, with more than two million Americans annually entering hospital and ending up with a totally different complaint to the one that caused them to seek treatment in the first place.

*

The heart beats faster during a heated argument than during sexual intercourse.

The most efficient machine in the universe is the human heart. The heart pumps the equivalent of 1,500,000 gallons a year, which during the average lifetime is enough to fuel more than 2000 Jumbo Jets!

*

To carry the blood to every part of the human body takes sixty thousand miles of blood vessels.

*

The function of the female Fallopian tubes was not fully discovered until the nineteenth century.

*

Until the end of the eighteenth century a very popular drug for every kind of ailment was powdered Egyptian Mummy. If someone was suffering from VD then powdered penis would be given as a cure.

*

The most durable organ of the human body is the liver. If seventy-five per cent of your liver were taken away the remaining twenty-five per cent would continue to function quite happily, and after a time the liver would build itself up again to its original size – the only organ to do this.

*

In 1978 the Israeli government opened a unique hospital – the world's largest camel hospital. In a country where camels are essential to the economy, the million-dollar clinic has become a necessity for sick camels.

*

After the invention of the X-ray in 1895, London shops began to sell for the first time X-ray proof underwear so that it would be impossible for anyone to look at your 'private parts' without your authority.

The Hunza tribe of north-west Kashmir are medical record breakers in that they are the only people in the world who do not suffer from cancer.

*

Japanese women are the only women in the world who voluntarily have fifty inches of their large intestine removed. This is for cosmetic reasons – their skin turns from yellow to white.

*

The 'longest' disease known to man is a lung disease called: PNEUMONOULTRAMICROSCOPICSSILICOVOL-CANOCONIOSIS.

*

In 1963 Dr Chen Chung-Wei in Shanghai performed the first successful operation to reattach a completely severed hand.

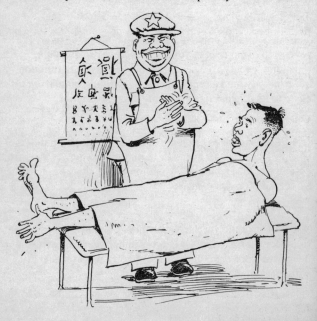

Ovarian cysts are the most bizarre of human growths and can contain surprising objects such as teeth and hair, although doctors cannot understand how they come to be there. There is the case of an eighteen-year-old girl on record who was found to have a large ovarian cyst that contained 150 teeth. Although less common there are cases of similar growths being found in men's testicles.

*

In 1976 psychologists in Wisconsin, USA, did a study on male urinations. Monitoring a public lavatory and the flows of urine they discovered that the speed, volume of urine, and length of time a man spends in the urinal is affected by the number of other people present and their proximity to him.

*

The first cataract operations were performed thousands of years ago using thorns to remove the 'web' from the eye. There are detailed accounts of such operations being performed in India in 1000 BC, at a time when if the surgeon was not successful he lost a hand. There was, therefore, a limit to how many mistakes a surgeon could make – which must have been a comfort to the patient!

*

One of the rarest operations is that of sewing back a severed penis. There are only four recorded occasions on which this operation has been performed. The severed penis is restored to its original position in a seven-hour operation by skilled surgeons using modern microsurgical-techniques.

*

In an age of sex equality, by 1979 still less than ten per cent of surgeons were women.

*

In the United Kingdom forty-two per cent of the population (males and females) suffer regularly from headaches, the highest percentage in the world. It just might not always be an excuse for not having sex.

Medical studies record that more people catch colds through shaking hands than through kissing.

*

Heroin was discovered in 1890 and was thought to be a good cure for opium addiction.

*

Valium is the most widely used drug in the world.

*

The most common physical condition in the world is tooth decay. By the age of fifteen, more than ninety-five per cent of teenagers have some form of permanent decay in their teeth.

*

The longest anyone has remained constipated is 102 days.

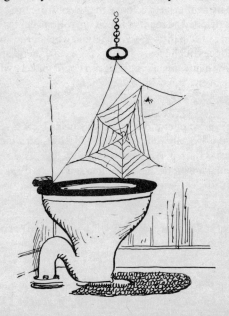

Victors and the Vanquished

'Join the army, see the world, meet interesting people and kill them.'

(Pacifist slogan 1970s)

In 1976 equatorial Guinea declared that it would be compulsory for all boys between seven and fourteen to undergo a period of military training. Any parent not agreeing to this 'will be shot'.

*

A fourteenth century Serbian prince called Marks Krayleric is said to have killed 1000 Turkish soldiers with a sword 1.82m (6 ft) long and weighing 22.6 kg (50 lbs).

*

Laos has been the most heavily bombed country in the world. Between May 1964 and February 1973, as the supply route to South Vietnam, two-and-a-half million tons of bombs were dropped on the country.

*

Sergeant Hawthorne, an early twentieth century British army instructor, could support a 400 lb (181.43 kg) gun on his shoulder and hold it there whilst it was fired.

Twelve hundred people were killed in anti-conscription riots in New York in 1863.

*

The British forces launched eight attacks over 102 days at the Battle of Passchendaele in 1917. In that time they advanced five miles for the loss of 400,000 men.

*

Nearly 649,000 jeeps were manufactured during the Second World War. At peak production one jeep was completed every eighty seconds.

*

In 1944 war expenditure reached its peak and at times was costing the British Government over £1000 milion per week.

*

The earliest guns took so long to load that it is said that bows and arrows were twelve times more efficient.

*

A record number of soldiers are still missing after the Second World War, with some 500,000 still unaccounted for and there are an equal number of civilians who disappeared and have never returned.

*

Staff-sergeant Alfred Moss could cut the thread supporting a lemon with his sword and then slice the fruit twice before it hit the ground.

*

The War of Jenkins' Ear was so-called because Captain Robert Jenkins in 1738 displayed his own pickled ear in a jar before Parliament, and claimed that it had been lopped off by a Spaniard. As a result Britain declared war on Spain!

The bloodiest civil war in history was the T'ai-p'ing Rebellion fought in China from 1851 to 1864, led by the psychopathic leader Hung Hsiu-ch'tian, in which an estimated 30,000,000 people died.

*

The bloodiest British battle on record is the Battle of Towton, fought in March 1461, when 36,000 Yorkists attacked 40,000 Lancastrians and won. The total death toll may have been 38,000 men, exactly fifty per cent of the soldiers who took part in the battle.

*

Until 1879 British soldiers convicted of bad conduct were tattooed with the initials 'BC'.

*

The bloodiest battle this century was the Battle of the Somme, fought from 1 July to 19 November 1916, with 1,300,000 lives lost.

*

Most countries have been at war with each other at some time in the history of the world, all except England and Portugal between whom there is the longest peace between nations.

*

Those who lived through the Second World War, which broke out on 3 September 1939, are in for a shock – the war isn't officially over! Germany and the Soviet Union never signed a peace treaty.

*

In 1815 after the Battle of Waterloo the Duke of York had a corridor of his home lined with the teeth of horses which had been killed in battle.

During the first battle of the Somme in 1916 the sound of gun-fire could be heard on Hampstead Heath.

*

Deaths during the Second World War were higher than any other war in the entire history of the world, with the final toll being around 60,000,000 dead.

*

One of the most accurate predictions about war was that of the author Stephen Southwold who predicted that the Second World War would break out on 3 September, 1939, in his book *Valiant Clay* which was published in 1931.

*

Soldiers in Ancient Greece went into battle naked from the waist down.

Wild Wild Women

'Sire, Four virgins wait without.'
'Without what?'
'Without food and clothing.'
'Give them food and bring them in.'

Anon.

Among her many lovers – who included Gary Cooper, Eddie Cantor, and Hollywood's first Dracula, Bela Lugosi – Clara Bow, the 'It' girl, is reputed to have entertained the entire University of Southern California's 1927 football team.

*

Queen Zingus, a seventeenth century sovereign in Angola, was one of the most sadistic nymphomaniacs ever to have lived. She kept a large harem well stocked with the finest specimens of masculinity that her kingdom could provide. She enjoyed arranging gladiatorial battles between her warriors, bedding the victor, and she regularly had her lovers executed on the morning after the night before.

*

In 1922 Therese Vaughan admitted to an astonished courtroom in Sheffield that she had married sixty-one husbands during the past five years. These men had been acquired in England, Germany and South Africa at the rate of about one a month.

*

Shan-Yin, a princess of the Sung dynasty in China, ordered a special bed to be made that could accommodate herself and thirty lovers at one time.

*

The earliest known orgasm in a female is three months.

*

One in fourteen adult women never experience orgasm.

*

Ninety-five per cent of women reach orgasm if intercourse continues for over sixteen minutes, ninety-two per cent if foreplay continues for twenty minutes.

*

The greatest number of separate orgasms experienced by one woman is twelve in one hour.

The greatest number of recorded successful caesarean births is thirteen by a woman in Ireland.

*

Four babies are born every second, but the chances of a mother giving birth to quadruplets are about 1 in 600,000.

*

The first female pharoah was Queen Hatshepsut in 1502 BC, but so as not to cause too great a shock all her official portraits and statues gave her a beard and tactfully forgot to give her breasts.

*

A survey in the USA revealed that more women meet prospective lovers whilst shopping than they do in bars and restaurants.

*

To cure her husband of 'the fever' in the sixteenth century, there is a case recorded of a woman who fed him crushed 'Spanish Fly', a known aphrodisiac. They then made love eighty-seven times in succession. The husband died from gangrene of the penis.

*

In the year 1852 when the first public lavatories for women were opened in London, only twenty-four women used them in the first twelve months.

*

The monastery on Mount Athos in Greece is one of the few places where a woman has never been, even though it is dedicated to the Virgin Mary.

*

The greatest number of twins born to one woman is four sets. The odds against this happening are 65,610,000 to 1.

The woman who has appeared on the cover of *Time* magazine more than any other – ten times in all – is the Virgin Mary.

*

Only the female mosquito bites. Male mosquitoes are vegetarian.

*

The first woman to test a rocket plane was pilot Hanna Reitsch, a German woman who is said to have flown to Berlin to rescue Hitler only to discover that he had just committed suicide. It is also said that during her life she broke almost every bone in her body through flying accidents.

*

Many jokes suggest that women talk more than men, but as infants it is generally male babies that are the first to learn to speak.

*

In the nineteenth century the most popular 'prescription' for a woman to enlarge her breasts was to rub them with fresh stawberries.

*

A 1971 survey in Britain revealed that for every man in a mental institution there are thirty-five women.

*

A survey at the same time on prisons showed that for every woman in jail there are thirty-five men, so more men commit crimes than women, but more women go mad than men!

*

An American woman, Margaret Sanger, in 1917 opened the first birth control clinic, and as a result was sent to the workhouse for a month.

The most startling record of an abdominal pregnancy is that of a seventy-five-year-old woman from Alabama. When she died after an operation a fully grown foetus was discovered in her abdomen at the post-mortem. The foetus was calcified and had been there for some twenty-five years without the woman realising it. The foetus was not, incidentally, the cause of death – she was shot by a member of her family during an argument!

*

There are no known great female composers. List any of the famous classical composers from Beethoven to Bach, Tchaikovsky to Stravinsky – they are all men.

*

The woman with the longest hair in Britain is Irena Godyn, whose hair is over seventy-six inches long. She says it takes her one whole bottle of shampoo every time she washes it.

The female sea cow has breasts just like a human female and suckles her young in exactly the same way. When excited she makes a crying sound which could be mistaken for singing, and the combination of these attributes have probably brought about the myth of mermaids, for in the dim light and at a distance that is exactly what the sea cow appears to be.

*

In Britain the odds against a girl marrying a millionaire are twenty-five thousand to one. Sorry girls!

*

Women making fire extinguishers in American wartime factories believed that the carbon tetrachloride they were using made them pregnant.

*

Nuns living in a close-knit community like a convent, with no male contact whatsoever, all menstruate at exactly the same time. This also happens, although less frequently, in hospitals where nurses all have their periods together. It is thought to have something to do with 'odour', although no real research has yet been done.

*

Marie de Medici, Queen of France, owned a dress which at present day prices would cost £6 million. She only wore it once.

*

The average American woman kisses seventy-nine men before marriage.

*

Corsets were worn by fourteenth century French ladies as an outer-garment, not an under-garment as today.

One of the earliest forms of beauty treatment to relieve a woman of her double chins was to place a strap under her jaw and hoist her into the air.

*

Extensive studies reveal that women are less likely to fall out of bed than men.

X = Censorship

'What most men desire is a virgin who is a whore.'

Edward Dahlberg

A 1974 survey showed that thirty-two per cent of boys, and sixteen per cent of girls, had had sexual intercourse before the age of sixteen.

*

Eleven out of twelve sexually active teenagers now use some form of contraception.

*

One million teenagers in America become pregnant each year; sixty per cent give birth.

*

Over 300,000 teenagers in the USA obtain abortions for unwanted pregnancies every year.

*

The two most serious and commonly transmitted sexual diseases are gonorrhoea and syphillis. Today these are more likely to be picked up by having sex with a friend than by having sex with a prostitute.

*

Gonorrhoea is the world's second most common infectious disease, (measles is more common), with 200 million people infected each year.

*

The word 'sex' made its first appearance in print in Wycliffe's translation of the Bible which was printed in 1380.

*

London's Wig Club, which flourished for over a hundred years from the middle of the sixteenth century took its name from a most unusual hairpiece: a wig woven from the pubic hair of King Charles II's several mistresses. Every prospective member of the club was obliged to supply a lock of his own mistress' hair so that it could be added to the original wig.

The world famous psycho-kineticist, Uri Geller, was threatened with a law-suit by an irate Swedish girl, who blamed him for her unwanted pregnancy. She claimed that his unusual powers were responsible for bending her contraceptive device when she and her fiancé were making love whilst watching Mr Geller on television.

*

In Georgian England the testicles of all animals were used as aphrodisiacs, the lion's testicles being considered the most powerful and potent.

*

Samuel Pepys indulged himself in an unusual treat on his thirty-sixth birthday. He went to Westminster Abbey and kissed the embalmed body of Henry V's queen, Catherine de Valois, who had been dead for over 200 years.

Canes used to give corporal punishment in many London schools are, a 1977 investigation revealed, bought in a Soho sex shop.

*

In the mid-nineteenth century all Turkish newspapers were censored. When the King and Queen were murdered the newspapers stated that they had died from indigestion.

*

The male spider's penis is located at the end of one of its legs.

*

In Hamburg today a multi-storey brothel is the only one of its kind to be accepted by the authorities.

*

Cleopatra is credited with taking on 100 men a night, Catherine the Great advocated sex six times a day as a cure for insomnia and more modestly Brigitte Bardot once asserted that she 'must have a man every night'.

*

Bacteria can reproduce sexually.

*

A Rhode Island law proposed that sex should be taxed. A two dollar tax was levied on every act of sexual intercourse.

*

Pornography is a four-billion dollar business in the USA annually.

*

The people of Trastevere, near Rome, speak a dialect all of their own and have over two thousand words for the human sex organs.

The legal term for committing adultery is 'criminal conversation'.

*

Three of the world's greatest sailors, Christopher Columbus, Ferdinand Magellan and Captain Cook, all suffered from syphillis.

*

After being injured in a car crash an Australian man found that he was unable to kiss because his lips had been left numb. He was awarded 142,000 dollars in damages.

*

In India sex shops are officially registered as 'museums'.

*

The first striptease was an impromptu divestment at the Paris Four Arts Ball in 1893. Its effect was so devastating that it led to a riot in the Latin Quarter and the besieging of the prefecture of police.

*

It is a fallacy to believe that great debauchees wear themselves out and die young. August of Saxony-Poland, respectfully surnamed 'the strong', died at sixty-three, Catherine the Great at sixty-seven and Casanova at seventy-three.

*

Abbotsholme School in England in 1889 became the first school to give sex education.

*

What the English call a 'French Letter', the French call an 'English Letter'.

Apart from his deformed, hunchback physique Toulouse Lautrec suffered from a complaint which gave him an excessively large penis. The girls in the brothel where he lived nicknamed him 'teapot'.

*

The world's oldest sperm (fertile) survived twenty-five years. It was a sample of bull's sperm frozen in 1952 and thawed out in 1977 to celebrate the Queen's Silver Jubilee. The results of this experiment has led to greater research into freezing human sperm for sperm banks and experiments with test-tube babies.

*

The oldest surviving contraceptive sheaths are made from dried sheep's gut. Their efficiency was so doubtful that even the manufacturers advised wearing two.

In Israel Jews may listen to women singing on the radio, providing it isn't a love song and they don't personally know the woman.

*

The British 'X' certificate was introduced in 1951.

You Won't Believe It!

'The best contraceptive device in the world
is a glass of cold water;
not before or after, but instead.'

Anon.

3500 houses in Chicago, USA, are piped methane gas made from cow dung. The Calorific Recovery Anaerobic Process Inc. are responsible for producing this gas – their acronym being C.R.A.P.

*

Turkey had to wait longer than any other country to be electrified. This is because the Sultan heard that dynamos would be used and, thinking they were associated with dynamite, vetoed the project.

*

St Nicholas, popularly known as 'Santa Claus', is the patron saint of thieves.

*

In America 170,000,000 telephones have been installed, of which 25,000,000 are ex-directory.

*

Three thousand Indians die every year from their own homemade alcohol. As they use swamp water and dead rats in the process it is not surprising!

*

A diamond may be the hardest substance known to man, but it was discovered by accident in the seventeenth century that if a diamond is heated enough – it melts, and will burn like carbon.

*

Japanese farmers improve their sex lives by drinking a potion made with dead earthworms.

Surveys prove that the average person's right shoe wears out faster than their left.

*

At any given moment there are 1800 thunderstorms somewhere in the world and lightning is striking the earth 100 times a second.

*

One of the luckiest women alive is a Kansas lady whose house was hit by a tornado on 10 June, 1958. It lifted her sixty feet in the air and dropped her beside her record player. The record on the turntable was . . . *Stormy Weather*.

*

In 1975 forty karate experts at Chesterfield, England, demolished twelve houses – with their hands and feet.

Eighteen-month-old Mathew Williams from Worcestershire was run over by a car. The wheels went right over him. He escaped without a single cut or bruise.

*

The most common first name in the world is Mohammed.

*

Svangerskabsforebyggendermiddel is the Danish word for contraceptive.

*

A Great Dane called 'Caliph' made legal history. Whilst on trial for his life, he bit the judge.

*

Psychologists report that fifteen per cent of the population secretly chew their toenails.

The largest iceberg on record was the size of Belgium.

*

People have been struck by many objects falling from the sky, but few have had the experience of an elderly African woman who in 1978 was hit on the head by a dog.

*

The longest word ever said on a single record is: TAUMATAWHAKATANGIHANAKOAUQUOTA-MATEATURIPUKAKPIKIMAUNCAHORONUKUPO KAIWHENUAKITANATAHU! The record was called *The Lone Ranger* and was recorded in 1977 by Quantum Jump.

*

The greatest morale-booster possible for a hippopotamus is to defecate more copiously than any rival hippo. Sounds like a real ego-trip!

*

Sixteenth century Irish saint, Brigid of Kildare, did not change water into wine, but had the power to transform her dirty bathwater into beer for visiting members of the clergy.

*

Chinese girls believe that they can get pregnant by swimming in a public pool.

*

The Ancient Chinese held a belief that sperm came from the brain.

*

If you have an IQ of 180 it is a record! You will be literally one in a million.

Urine was the first form of toothpaste.

*

In India the Chench Tribe believed that to have sex in the dark will result in blind children.

*

The population of the world is increasing by one-and-a-half million people every week.

*

Casualty figures reveal that more people die each year after being kicked to death by a donkey than are killed in plane crashes.

*

The greatest recorded number of 'husbands' eaten by a black widow spider is twenty-five in one day.

*

The slowest creatures to have sex are snails! They mate just once in a lifetime, and the longest recorded mating between two adult snails lasted twelve hours.

*

If you were born in January, February or March you are more likely to be schizophrenic than if you were born at any other time.

*

The most embarrassing masturbation recorded is that of a man (who wishes to remain anonymous!) who whilst working in a dairy attached his penis to the automatic milking machine and was unable to remove it. The protein content of the cream was said to be much higher than usual . . .

The original juggernaut was a huge idol of the Hindu god Krishna, which used to be dragged through the streets once a year. The more devout worshippers used to commit suicide by throwing themselves under the trailer which carried the statue.

*

Of the land on the earth the largest part, more than one-sixth, is owned by the Soviet Union.

*

The Lhopa tribe in Tibet used to celebrate a marriage by eating the bride's mother at the wedding feast, a custom many Englishmen would like to continue!

In twenty-five years a clan of fifteenth century Scottish cannibals reputedly killed and ate 1000 people.

Zoo's Best

'All animals are equal, but some animals
are more equal than others.'

George Orwell

'The fly ought to be used as the symbol of
impertinence and audacity; for whilst all
other animals shun man more than anything else,
and run away even before he comes
near them, the fly lights upon his very nose.'

Schopenhauer

The duck-billed platypus does not have nipples. Milk oozes out of pores in its abdomen.

*

If you thought that giraffes are big-hearted creatures, then you wouldn't be far wrong because giraffes have the largest heart of any land animal. A giraffe's heart is two feet long and weighs up to twenty-five pounds.

*

Giraffes have the highest blood pressure in the world. Because they have such long necks, it takes a lot of pressure to pump blood to their brains, which may be as much as twelve feet away from their hearts.

*

A butterfly's eye has 17,000 lenses, each one possessing the optical power of a single eye.

*

There is approximately one rat in the British Isles for every person living in the country.

*

Baboons are so intelligent that the ancient Egyptians trained them to wait at table. It is quite feasible, therefore, to say that the waiters in your favourite restaurant have about as much intelligence as a baboon!

*

One of the smallest creatures to be born in relation to its adult size is the panda. A baby panda when it is born weighs less than four ounces and is smaller than a mouse.

*

The digestive juices of a crocodile are so strong that six-inch nails can be dissolved.

A blue whale calf weighs ten tonnes at birth and achieves sexual maturity at the age of two and a half.

*

A parrot's beak can snap shut with a force of 350 pounds per square inch.

*

The tallest bird ever known was the flightless New Zealand moa, that attained a height of approximately eleven feet. It died out in the sixteenth century.

*

The gestation period of a rhinoceros is 560 days, which is a long time to be pregnant!

*

The largest ant colony is in a forest in the Jura Mountains. Experts estimate that some three hundred million ants live here in twelve hundred different anthills which appear to be joined together by a network of ant-sized roads.

*

All polar bears are left-handed.

*

The most dangerous fish known to man is the electric eel which can discharge over 400 volts. Shocking indeed!

*

Alpine salamanders are pregnant for over three years, and always give birth to twins.

*

The elephant is the only animal with four knees.

Oysters are ambisexual. This means that they can change from being a male to a female several times during their lives.

*

Ninety-nine per cent of all life forms that have existed on the earth are now completely extinct.

*

The first elephant twins were born to an elephant in Tanzania in 1976.

*

A flea can jump 200 times its own length. Its jump has been likened to a man jumping from a kneeling position to the top of the Post Office Tower thirty thousand times.

*

A mosquito has forty-seven teeth.

*

The sex of a glow worm can be told by the number of flashes it emits. Male glow worms send out a pulse of light once every six seconds, a female once every two seconds.

*

Disease-spreading ticks can live for up to twenty-five years, can survive five years without food, each female tick can lay eight thousand eggs, and they all live by sucking blood.

*

The reproductive system of a cat is similar to that of a human female, but the male cat has sharp tufts on his penis which scratch the female when he withdraws after intercourse, causing the female to yowl with pain. The cat's penis probably scratches the vagina and starts the ovulation.

The largest massacre by animals occurred in February 1945 when 1000 Japanese soldiers were wading waist deep through a Burmese swamp. Crocodiles from miles around moved in for the kill. Only a hundred men survived.

*

The slowest animal of all is the sloth, which has a maximum speed of one mile in four hours. It hangs lethargically in trees, and is said only to excrete when it rains – and always from its position high up in the trees. Sex is always haphazard with both the male and female hanging upside down for a long time, each waiting for the other to make the first move!

*

Fireflies are bright enough to shine through the stomach of a frog.

*

The last wild wolf was sighted in Britain in 1864, but an official wolf-catcher is still employed in Yorkshire to scare away any wild wolves. The annual wage for this honour is two pounds.

*

The only animals to have identity cards are 300,000 cows in Israel.

*

Killer bees have stung more than 300 people to death in Brazil in the last twenty years. In an attack the bees swarm on to one person and sting at a rate of sixty times a minute. Such an attack can last up to two hours, but the person is usually dead after 500 stings.

A chameleon has a longer tongue in relation to the size of its body than any other animal, its tongue being twice the length of its entire body.

*

The Australian 'possum' first appeared on the earth 45 million years ago and is one of the oldest species of animal.

*

The only animals that can crawl along a razor blade without cutting themselves are snails. They secrete a sticky discharge which enables them to slide over anything – which is why snails leave a slimy trail behind them.

*

There are approximately
3,000,000,000,000,000,000,000,000,000,000,000
animals on the earth, not including man.

*

The giant squid has the largest eyeball of any living animal, being the same diameter as a long-playing record, approximately 38cm (15 in) across.

*

The longest living mammal, having been known to attain an age of 115, is a two-legged creature called *Homo sapiens*.

*

The female praying mantis after having mated with the male, then proceeds to devour him whole.

The lammergeier, or bearded vulture as it is commonly known, is the only bird of prey to eat bone marrow. It flies into the air with a bone in its beak, and drops it onto rocks from a great height so that it can get at the marrow.

*

The starfish is the only animal to have an eye on the end of each arm.

*

The silkworm moth has eleven brains.

LEONARD ROSSITER

THE LOWEST FORM OF WIT

Sarcasm is the lowest form of wit – no one is beneath using it – but it is also the most satisfying. There is no greater pleasure than pinning your squirming victim to the dinner-table with a carefully sharpened and coolly aimed insult or flooring him with a sudden and crippling kick beneath the belt.

Sarcasm requires deadly accuracy and perfect timing. It is the most skilful kind of unarmed combat and because no holds are barred it is also the most dangerous. THE LOWEST FORM OF WIT is a complete handbook for aspiring masters and mistresses of sarcasm compiled by Leonard Rossiter, a black belt of this vicious art. He tells you everything you need to know about sarcasm from its low-down role in history to specific advice on dealing with traffic wardens, bank managers, neighbours, foreigners and other despicable persons.

This is a treasury of biting jibes and stinging retorts which explores the lowest kind of wit in the highest kind of style.

HUMOUR   0 7221 7513 2   £1.50

TONIGHT
JOSEPHINE

and other undiscovered letters
Michael Green
IF . . .

Julius Caesar had gone for a picnic and left the Senate to have a stab at something else

Hitler had taken his ever-loving mother's advice about his friends (especially the fat one)

Archimedes' plumbing had got him into hot water

Napoleon had had more than wandering hand trouble

. . . History would have been very, very different!

Here at last are the letters which changed the world (or would have if they'd ever been written).

'Delightfully engaging . . . could prove even more popular than his huge successes *The Art of Coarse Rugby, The Art of Coarse Sailing,* etc.'
Sunday Express

HUMOUR   0 7221 4084 3   £1.25

MEN
EXASPERATING TO LIVE WITH.
IMPOSSIBLE TO LIVE WITHOUT.

The Classified MAN

TWENTY-TWO TYPES OF MEN
(and what to do about them)

Susanna M. Hoffman

Look out for:—

The Instant Barricader – he comes on like a hurricane and disappears just as fast.

The Idle Lord – he believes that money was made to be spent – *yours* on *him*.

The Man Who Would Be Mogul – he lives solely for business. All other things – women, children, friends, holocausts, funerals – come second.

Recognise somebody? If not, you'll certainly find him between the covers of Ms. Hoffman's hilarious book. A book that no women should be without.

GENERAL   0 7221 4603 5   £1.50

A selection of bestsellers from SPHERE

FICTION

THE SKULL BENEATH THE SKIN	P. D. James	£1.95 ☐
WINGS OF THE MORNING	David and Betty Beaty	£2.95 ☐
THE RED DOVE	Derek Lambert	£1.95 ☐
DOMINA	Barbara Wood	£2.50 ☐
A PERFECT STRANGER	Danielle Steel	£1.75 ☐

FILM & TV TIE-INS

BY THE SWORD DIVIDED	Mollie Hardwick	£1.75 ☐
THE DOCTOR WHO TECHNICAL MANUAL	Mark Harris	£2.50 ☐
YELLOWBEARD	Graham Chapman and David Sherlock	£2.50 ☐
THE KIDS FROM FAME 2	Lisa Todd	£1.75 ☐

NON-FICTION

MONEYWOMAN	Georgina O'Hara	£1.75 ☐
THE FINAL DECADE	Christopher Lee	£2.50 ☐
A QUESTION OF BALANCE	H.R.H. The Duke of Edinburgh	£1.50 ☐
SUSAN'S STORY	Susan Hampshire	£1.75 ☐
SECOND LIFE	Stephani Cook	£1.95 ☐

All Sphere books are available at your local bookshop or newsagent, or can be ordered direct from the publisher. Just tick the titles you want and fill in the form below.

Name _____

Address _____

_____

Write to Sphere Books, Cash Sales Department, P.O. Box 11, Falmouth, Cornwall TR10 9EN

Please enclose a cheque or postal order to the value of the cover price plus:

UK: 45p for the first book, 20p for the second book and 14p for each additional book ordered to a maximum charge of £1.63.

OVERSEAS: 75p for the first book and 21p per copy for each additional book.

BFPO & EIRE: 45p for the first book, 20p for the second book plus 14p per copy for the next 7 books, thereafter 8p per book.

Sphere Books reserve the right to show new retail prices on covers which may differ from those previously advertised in the text or elsewhere, and to increase postal rates in accordance with the PO.